THE DAY OF THE CRESCENT

CONSTANTINOPLE

From Grelot's *Voyage de Constantinople*, 1680

THE DAY OF THE CRESCENT

GLIMPSES OF OLD TURKEY

BY

G. E. HUBBARD

LATELY H.M. VICE-CONSUL FOR THE VILAYET OF MOSUL
Author of *From the Gulf to Ararat*

CAMBRIDGE
AT THE UNIVERSITY PRESS
1920

CAMBRIDGE
UNIVERSITY PRESS

University Printing House, Cambridge CB2 8BS, United Kingdom

Published in the United States of America by Cambridge University Press, New York

Cambridge University Press is part of the University of Cambridge.

It furthers the University's mission by disseminating knowledge in the pursuit of education, learning and research at the highest international levels of excellence.

www.cambridge.org
Information on this title: www.cambridge.org/9781107679290

© Cambridge University Press 1920

First published 1920
First paperback edition 2014

A catalogue record for this publication is available from the British Library

ISBN 978-1-107-67929-0 Paperback

PREFACE

THIS book issues from the press on the eve of the conclusion of the Turkish Peace Treaty. The occasion lends an added piquancy to the subject. Turkey in defeat contrasts with Turkey triumphant and the gulf between gives the measure of a nation's fall.

The Treaty, unless all the signs are at fault, will reduce a straggling and divided Empire to a compact and unified State, and launch Turkey on a new era of existence as an ethnical unit. Her development on these new lines will profoundly affect the course of history in the Nearer East and will certainly be watched keenly by all who study the trend of events in that quarter of the globe. In this class of readers one may safely postulate a retrospective interest in the nation's past, and to them I confidently commend this humble attempt to create a picture of the golden age of Turkey.

For the rest, my aim will be rewarded if the book makes an appeal to the sense we all possess for the exotic and picturesque, while throwing a little fresh light on the history and character of a people whom Englishmen have found worthy of their steel ever since the days when first they met

> "in glorious Christian field,
> Streaming the ensign of the Christian cross
> Against black pagans, Turks, and Saracens."
> (*Richard II*, IV. I.)

I am indebted to the editor of *The United Services Magazine* for permission to incorporate in this book the greater part of an article entitled " The Fighting Turk " which I contributed to a recent issue, and I have to acknowledge the courtesy of the Hakluyt Society in agreeing to use being made of the Society's reprints of the Covel and Dallam diaries.

Professor E. G. Browne has most kindly corrected the proofs of the book with a view to the orthography of oriental names and words, and Mr Wratislaw, His Majesty's Consul-General at Beyrout, and a direct descendant of the Baron Wratislaw who figures in the book as the hero of the last two chapters, has given me most useful assistance in revising the text.

G. E. H.

April, 1920

CONTENTS

CHAPTER IV

CHAPTER V

CHAPTER VI

CHAPTER VII

CHAPTER VIII

CHAPTER IX

CHAPTER X

CHAPTER XI

CHAPTER XII

CHAPTER XIII

LIST OF ILLUSTRATIONS

INTRODUCTION

A year ago, while delving among some of the dustiest bookshelves of the Foreign Office library, I happened on a row of ancient books on Turkey bound for the most part in decrepit leather bindings with a faded, but illustrious, coat-of-arms stamped on their covers. They proved on closer inspection to belong to a collection bequeathed some time in the last century by a noble diplomat who, when attached to the Constantinople embassy, had made a hobby of collecting books on Turkish travel of the sixteenth and seventeenth centuries. Having been myself a sojourner and traveller in Turkey, my curiosity was roused by these time-worn records from an earlier age and I dipped into them with an idle interest, to find myself rapidly engrossed in a quite fascinating study.

The authors were a cosmopolitan and heterogeneous lot, including among others such diverse characters as a Flemish diplomat, a French artist, a Polish soldier, a Venetian dragoman and an English man of science. Their stories of how they travelled, painted, plotted or fought according to their several capacities are full of colour and romance and worthy products of the age of adventure in which the actors lived. The old-fashioned letterpress and quaint woodcuts which adorn their pages opened the door, moreover, into what was to me—as I venture to think it will be to most of my readers—an almost unexplored subject, the "Golden Age" of Turkey. No writer has given us a Rise and Fall of the *Ottoman* Empire, or painted the life of Constantinople in the great days of the Turk as Gibbon painted it under the Byzantine emperors. Modern histories of Turkey rarely descend to picturesque detail and even the homely, discursive works of old Richard Knollys and Sir Paul Rycaut penetrate but seldom beyond the regions of affairs of state. These old travel-books, on the other hand, raise the curtain on the Turkish life of their day in all its intimate aspects. The stage is crowded with picturesque figures—the proud and petulant Janissary, the naked, screaming dervish, the "three-tail" Pasha with his train of "catamites" and extravagant suite, the wild, undisciplined Tartar, the Grand Vizir risen from a swineherd to the highest post in the Empire and the "Grand Turke" himself challenging Christendom, with a sublime contempt for all brother kings and emperors. The scenes among which the actors play are besides of infinite variety, ranging the scale from the dazzling splendours of the Grand Signior's court to the unspeakable horrors of life in the slave-galleys.

I have tried, by a process of selection and compression, to fit the most interesting parts of these old narratives into the pages of the present book, and have aimed at doing so in such a way as to give as general a picture as possible of the unique military and political system which the Turks had developed when they reached the summit of their power. It is easy to forget how great that power was and what an immense menace the Turks, with their incomparable military organization, laid upon the rest of Europe during the period with which we have to deal. One need only look at the many references to the Turks in Shakespeare's plays to realize how much the Turkish peril obsessed the minds of our Elizabethan ancestors. A couple of instances taken from contemporary publications may not be out of place.

In the preface of Knollys's *Historie of the Turkes* published in 1610, we come on the following dirge "The Long and still declining state of the Christian Commonwealthe with the dishonour done unto the blessed name of Oure Savioure, the desolation of the Church militant here on Earth, the dreadfull dangers daily threatened unto the poor remainder thereof, the millions of souls cast headlong into eternal destruction, the infinity of woefull Christians whose grievous groans under the heavy yoke of Infidelity no tongue is able to express, might worthily move even a stonie heart to ruth and give just cause to any good Christian to sit downe and, with the heavie prophet, to say 'Oh, how hath the Lord darkened the Daughter of Zion in His wrath and cast downe from Heaven unto Earth the beautie of Israel!'" Even allowing that Knollys—a Fellow of Lincoln College and, generally speaking, a well-balanced writer—may have been something of an alarmist, one can hardly doubt that his dismal forebodings of the overwhelming of Christendom by the oncoming Turk reflected to a great extent the current feeling of his day.

The second instance may help to explain how this fear of the Turk came to be deeply implanted by showing us the astonishing attitude which the Sultan of Turkey felt able to adopt in his dealings with Christian monarchs. It is taken from a pamphlet published in London "at the Sign of the White Swan" in 1606, giving an English translation of "A letter of the Great Turke recently sent to all the Kings and Princes of Christendom." The letter is too long to quote in full, but the tenor of it is as follows:

Sultan Ahmed, "Shadow of God upon Earth, Barron of Turkie, Lord of the Upper and Lower Seas, Beloved in Heaven"—with a dozen more titles in a similar strain —calls upon the Great Champion of Rome (*alias* the Pope) and his Confederates, the Princes of Christendom, to submit themselves to his will and manifest their surrender by homages and tribute.

If they obey "and open their Townes and Gates," the Sultan will of his clemency suffer them to retain their faith and "accustomed ceremonies," but if they resist, then let them expect "nought else but mortall warres and firing of cities, with greate occision and deathe both of olde and young." The Christian Princes are advised "to take example by the Great Souldan of Babylon, whom we spoiled of his dignitie and pursued unto deathe" (a bit of quite gratuitous perversion this, as the Turks had, as a matter of fact, just suffered a notable disaster at Bagdad at the hands of Shah Abbas and his Persians), and are warned that presently the whole world will bow down to Sultan Ahmed, whose armies "are even now marching through Hungarie to invade all Germanie and the noble countrie of France" and will shortly capture Rome, "whose gorgeous temples shall be used as was the temple of the Holy Sophie."

This wild braggadocio of the nineteen-year-old Sultan strikes absurdly enough on modern ears, but we can be sure that it held little of mirth for a generation to whom the Turk was a veritable bogy and who could never forget that thousands of their fellow-Christians were labouring and dying as slaves in the Turkish galleys.

In the various stories reproduced in this book one can hardly fail to be struck by the two leading characteristics which marked the Turk in the days of his prime—his inordinate love of display and his inherent "militarism." The first of these was, I think one may safely say, a borrowed characteristic. The Turk was a simple primitive creature when he first emerged on to the Anatolian plains to conquer a powerful empire. But his victory over the Greeks contained the seeds of his own ruin. The national failings which had weakened the Greek defence infected their conquerors, who soon acquired the true Byzantine taste for lavish show and voluptuous luxury. This, with its inevitable accompaniment of bribery and corruption, slowly undermined the government of Turkey in the succeeding centuries, sapping the virility of her leaders and changing the character of her sultans from hardy tribal chiefs to the most contemptible of debauched despots. The process of the disease is easily traceable in the series of narratives embodied in the present volume.

Militarism, on the contrary, was inbred from the start. The Turk has never regarded war as the devastating interlude which we are wont to consider it, but rather as a natural, and by no means undesirable, state. Until recent times the administration of Turkey was purely military and the usual distinctions between civil and military authority did not exist. To quote from Sir Charles Eliot's classical book on Turkey, "every Turk is born a soldier"; in fact the Ottoman race is essentially a race of fighters. The course of history has done much to abet their natural aptitude. Their early career was passed in tribal warfare. Before they had fairly subdued their primitive rivals, they embarked on a David and Goliath struggle against the Western Empire, and on finally capturing Constantinople they found themselves

faced by enemies in every direction. A Christian con-
federacy opposed them on one side, the Persians
threatened on the other, while at sea they were at constant warfare with the Italian maritime states. For
nearly three centuries they fought endless campaigns
against Austria and Venice, their hereditary enemies,
till with the consolidation of Russia a fresh and even
deadlier enemy entered the field. Their struggle with
Russia led on to the gradual disintegration of their vast
empire, resulting in the wars of liberation which have
lasted into the present century, only to be eclipsed in
our own time by the general Armageddon. Turkish
history, indeed, is one endless record of war—a fact
reflected in the very large part which military topics
occupy in the following pages.

The military "genius" and moral decadence which
this book thus illustrates have been the two great factors
in Turkey's existence, and the fate of the empire has
largely depended on the balance between them. On
the whole the latter has triumphed in spite of such brilliant exceptions even in modern times as the defence
of Plevna or the holding of San-i-yat and Achi Baba.
The disease contracted by the conquerors of Byzantium
sapped the strength of the race and hastened the close
of the brilliant epoch of Turkish history which it is my
object to present to the reader; but it has left the Anatolian peasant, the backbone of Turkey, almost untouched.
"*Baluk bashdan kokar*" says the Turkish proverb, "the
fish rots from the head"; we have yet to see if the Turk
will succeed in arresting the process downwards.

CHAPTER I

A LITTLE CONDENSED HISTORY

The stories of Turkish travels in the pages of this book all fall within a period beginning in the middle of the sixteenth century and lasting some 150 years.

This century and a half saw the acme of the Turks' power, the beginning of their downward course and the brief recovery which, like a St Luke's summer, broke with a short-lived burst of sunshine into the autumn of their decline. It also covered the fiercest phases of the struggle between Turkey and Christendom, including the two occasions when Europe was seriously threatened with a wholesale Ottoman invasion. It is, indeed, as dramatic a period of history as you well could find, besides playing an important part in the development of the whole of Eastern Europe.

The present chapter by no means aims at giving a serious *résumé* of the times—anything of the sort, even were it within the writer's compass, would be out of place in the conception of this book as a collection of picturesque sketches. But the sketches will be better for being fitted into place, so for the sake of such of my readers as are not familiar with von Hammer or Creasy, I will attempt to reconstruct a slight historical background for the events of the chapters which follow.

To gain a connected idea of the relations between Turkey and the countries of Europe, it is well to go back nearly a century before the beginning of our period to the years immediately after the Fall of Constantinople. That impressive event raised a thorough panic throughout Europe and seemed likely for a time to revive the old Crusading spirit. The most extraordinary scenes resulted from the efforts of various princes to rouse the enthusiasm of Christian chivalry and raise volunteers for fresh crusades. Michaud describes, for instance, in his history of the Crusades, a *fête* which took place in the course of a congress at Lille which Philip of Burgundy had convoked to set on foot an expedition. The proceedings began with *tableaux vivants* representing stirring classical scenes such as the Labours of Hercules and the Quest of the Golden Fleece, followed by a pageant in which a herald-at-arms carrying a pheasant (the emblem of bravery) ushered in an elephant led by a Saracen, with a "tower" on its back containing a lady in black (a type of the Christian Church) who recited inspiring verses. The knights who were present were so fired by the spectacle that they one and all swore by the lady never to rest again till they had met the Turk in mortal combat and performed some prodigy of valour against the foe of Christendom. Their ardour was rewarded by a lady in white with "Grâce dieu" in golden letters on her back who presented to them seven lovely damsels representing the cardinal virtues, whereupon the whole assembly went off together to sup and dance!

But such-like fantastic attempts to resuscitate the crusades had little effect. The old spirit had been too effectually smothered by the pagan influences of the Renaissance, and the chronic state of discord in Europe made co-operative action almost impossible. Pius II made a brave attempt to organise and lead an army against Constantinople, but only a moderate host of poor and badly equipped crusaders collected at the meeting-place at Ancona. The knights and barons had ignored his summons and the disappointed Pope died before the crusade could start. From this time forward it was left to the Knights of St John to champion the Cross against the Crescent.

It was symptomatic of the change of mind which had come over Europe that when Charles VIII invaded Italy the King of Naples appealed for help simultaneously to the Pope and the Sultan!

Leo X tried, it is true, to continue the work of Pius and again preached a crusade; but his calls to the faithful remained unheeded. The wars between Francis and Charles were absorbing the energies of Europe, the Reformation spirit was already abroad and Luther himself was preaching that the Turk was the Scourge of God and that it was impious to resist him.

Turkey's Christian neighbours had meanwhile enjoyed a breathing space since the whirlwind campaign of Mohammed the Conqueror and his predecessors, thanks to the diversion of Ottoman enterprise in other directions. Selim the First, the cruel warrior-poet, spent his reigning years in leading the Turkish armies to new fields of conquest in the South and East. He had added huge tracts of Asia and Northern Africa to the empire, had forced the Persians back beyond Tabriz, and had conquered Syria, Arabia and Egypt. His taking of Cairo had, incidentally, resulted in an event of prime importance to the future history of Turkey, the last of the line of Abbaside caliphs—a creature at that time in the hands of the Mameluke rulers of Egypt—having been "persuaded" to transfer his hereditary office, to-

gether with the treasured standard and other relics of
the Prophet, to the Sultan of Turkey who henceforward
became Caliph of Islam.

Such was broadly the position in 1520 when the Sultanate passed to Suleyman the Second, surnamed "the
Magnificent," in whose reign the period covered by this
book begins. It is noteworthy that the half-century
during which he governed Turkey was one of the most
prolific of famous monarchs that history can show. His
contemporaries on the thrones of Europe and Asia include Queen Elizabeth, François Premier, the Emperor
Charles the Fifth, Shah Ismail the restorer of Persia,
and Akbar, the greatest of the Great Moguls. Suleyman
can claim an honourable place among these historic
figures. He was a man of most versatile talents, a fine
general, a great administrator and a legislator of such
note that he won the title of "*Canuni*" (the "Lawgiver").
Besides his sterner qualities he was a generous patron
of the arts, a student and writer of history and in philo-
sophy a disciple of Aristotle. He was also a very great
builder, and it is to him that Constantinople owes its
most splendid edifice of post-conquest date, the great
Suleymanieh mosque.

In the chapter dealing with the travels of Busbequius
the reader will find a sketch of Suleyman in his old age;
in his earlier years he has been described by an Italian
writer as a tall, thin man with a complexion "as if
smoked," prominent brow, fine black eyes "più tosto
pietosi che crudeli," aquiline nose and a thin mouth
adorned by long moustaches and a forked beard. It
is the picture of a proud and unrelentless man, and
this Suleyman certainly was. He placed himself high
above all other crowned heads, refused to correspond

with them on equal terms and treated them on a level with his own Vizir. Generous he could be when occasion warranted, as he showed when de Lisle Adam and the remnant of his knights surrendered Rhodes after their heroic defence of the town. Far from wreaking vengeance on the garrison for the enormous losses which the siege had cost him, Suleyman was moved only with admiration for their gallantry, and as they trooped out of the town gate he sent for their leader and congratulated him in public. The knights were allowed to leave the islands with the honours of war, taking their belongings with them, and were even furnished with Turkish ships to transport them home to Europe. As a lasting mark of Suleyman's fine spirit on this occasion, the arms of many of the knights still remain, left intact by his orders, on the lintels of the houses which they abandoned to the Turks.

The capture of Rhodes which was the scene of this incident happened in the third year of Suleyman's reign. Having disposed of this advanced outpost of Christendom which had long been a sharp thorn in the Turk's side, the Sultan turned his attention to Europe; four years later he conquered Hungary and seven years later was besieging Vienna. Though the situation was saved by the brave Comte de Salm, the appalling *débâcle* which the Hungarians had met with at Mohacz and the narrowly averted irruption of the Turks into central Europe stirred the Pope to a last futile effort to raise a crusade. Clement VII, though a prisoner of the Germans in Rome, sent out a despairing cry to the Christian world to unite against the infidel and actually ordered the plate in all the churches in Italy to be sold to provide funds. The appeal fell on deaf ears, and Europe might easily have been overwhelmed by the Turk but for the intervention of fortune which distracted Suleyman's attention to the more urgent task of repelling a Persian invasion. The old bitter hatred between Sunnite and Shïite and the Shah's efforts to regain his lost territories held the Ottoman armies engaged on the eastern frontier over the critical period.

But although the Turks did not again in Suleyman's time come within sight of the walls of Vienna, they made repeated campaigns into Europe and continually advanced their northern frontier. Hungary remained in vassalage to Turkey and the Emperor Ferdinand's attempts to wrest it back, his failures to do so and efforts to come to a settlement with Suleyman were the occasion of the embassy of Busbequius whose adventures fill chapters v, vi and vii.

Meanwhile with the help of the famous admiral Khair-ed-Din Barbarossa, the Turkish empire was extended along the coast of Northern Africa till it included Tripoli and Algiers; the only serious check to Suleyman's Mediterranean ambitions being his failure to take Malta, to which island the Knights of St John had migrated after the loss of Rhodes.

At the same time that he was extending his power abroad Suleyman was busy with reorganisation at home. He split up the empire into *pashaliks* and *sanjaks*, the same divisions roughly as exist to-day, laid down a law for the *rayahs*, giving them for the first time the right to hold property, remodelled the criminal law, founded schools, endowed the *ulema* and indulged in advanced economic experiments as, for instance, the regulation of prices and wages. He granted the first "Capitulations" (mark again the arrogant term to express what was really a treaty) which were obtained by the French in 1535.

His end was dramatic. He was an old man of seventy when he marched into Europe for the last time, leading a campaign against the Emperor Maximilian II who had succeeded his old enemy Ferdinand two years before. He had been checked on his last campaign by the fortress of Szigeth and was resolved this time to take it. The place was garrisoned by 3000 troops under Nicolas Zriny. Suleyman with 50,000 men sat down to besiege it. For months Zriny held out in the citadel till all hope of relief had vanished. Then he made his memorable sortie. On the chosen day every gun in the place was lined up behind the gates and filled to the muzzle, the remaining stock of powder was collected in one huge mine and the garrison prepared for the final sortie. All the knights put on their finest robes and jewellery while Zriny armed himself with the keys of the castle and a purse with a hundred pieces of gold " so," he said, " that the man who lays me out shall not complain that his work is wasted." On the signal the gates were thrown suddenly open, all the guns discharged point-blank into the Turkish hosts outside and the knights charged out in a body. The tremendous numbers of the Turks bore them back within the citadel when the mine exploded involving Turk and Magyar alike in a mighty holocaust.

The city which had defied Suleyman and which he had sworn to capture was taken, but Suleyman himself knew nothing of it. For two days his lifeless corpse with open eyes and cheeks artificially reddened had sat in his tent propped upright on the *divan*. His Vizir and a few of his trusted servants were alone in the secret, which they hid from the outside world by allowing no break to occur in the ordinary daily routine. To all appearance reports were regularly made to the dead Sultan, meals served, messages received and sent. The moment that Szigeth fell the royal tent was struck and the royal carriage with the Emperor's person visible inside headed for Constantinople. Selim, the heir to the throne, had been privately warned and hastened to meet the returning army.

They met at Adrianople, where the Sultan's death was at last publicly announced; Selim was acclaimed emperor by the assembled troops and, the danger of civil war being passed, it was possible to proceed openly with the funeral arrangements and to carry Suleyman's remains to their last resting-place in his own tomb-mosque at the capital.

Fifty years later Suleyman's epitaph was written by Richard Knollys the English historian, who commemorates the great Sultan in the following verse:

Magnificent Soliman mounts his father's throne
With Christian slaughters formidable growne.
Rhodes, Naxos, Paros felt his crueltie
And the sweet waters of the Tyrrhenean sea.
Th' Hungarian territories he did invade,
And fierce attempts on fair Vienna made,
Till from the walls of Sigeth meanly come,
Th' aspiring tyrant crept to his long home.

The State archives of Vienna preserve a contemporary account of the adventures of one of Comte de Salm's officers at the siege of Vienna which is worth quoting as an example of the nobler traits of Suleyman and his officers. Count Christopher von Zedlitz, a Cornet in the Austrian army, was taken prisoner by the Turks in a skirmish outside Vienna. After trying without success to strip off his armour, his captors put him on a baggage-mule and carried him to Headquarters.

There he was brought to Ibrahim Pasha, the Grand Vizir, who gave orders that his cuirass should be removed, but as none of the Turks present understood the intricacies of plate-armour Count Christopher remained safely ensconced in his shell. Eventually he was interrogated by the Sultan himself. "To him," says the record, "Count Christopher made answer, that if assured of his life he would undo himself. When Ibrahim Pacha had given him such assurance, he showed the interpreter two little screws at the side, which being loosed, the cuirass came to its pieces, to the great wonder of the Turks.

"As the account of these things spread itself through the camp, much was said of the feats of this man-at-arms, and of his singular dexterity under his strange attire, and everyone was curious to see him, being, moreover, among the first who had been taken prisoners out of the city itself of Vienna. He was, therefore, ordered to exhibit himself in full cuirass, armed at all points for the fight, and to prove whether in this fashion he could, without vantage, lift himself from the ground. On the following day, mules and several kicking horses being produced, Count Christopher laid himself on the ground with his cuirass screwed, and rising nimbly, without any vantage, sprung on a horse, and this he repeated several times ; and then, with running and vaulting, afforded those hellhounds a princely spectacle of knightly exercises to their great admiration, and specially that of Ibrahim Pacha, who soon after took him to himself, and kept him safe in his own custody. Meanwhile, there came to him certain officers to frighten or to prove him, telling him to hold himself in readiness, for that the Pacha would do him right that same day. To these he answered, that as a Christian he was in truth not afraid of death, as one who, in honour of his Redeemer, in obedience to his sovereign, and in defence of his country, had prepared himself by prayer for death at any hour or instant, and hoped and believed most certainly to enjoy eternal joy and happiness through Christ; but, nevertheless, could not credit that such was the order of the Pacha, for he knew for certain that what the Pacha had promised he would perform like an honourable soldier. When this reached the Pacha, the longer he considered, the more he admired not only the knightly feats, but the noble spirit of this hero. When, also, Soliman himself asked him whether, if he should release him, he would still make war upon him, Count Christopher answered, undismayed, that if God and his Redeemer should grant him deliverance, he would while life lasted fight against the Turks more hotly than ever. Thereupon the Sultan replied, 'Thou shalt be free, my man, and make war on me as thou wilt for the rest of thy life.'

"The Pacha, however, kept him in good case while the siege lasted, namely, about a month; and in place of his cuirass gave him a dress of red velvet Tyrian stuff, which he wore and lay in night and day, and sent him from his own table meat and mixed drinks as daily prepared for himself, and even in course of time offered and gave him wine.

"When the assault took place, the Count was left in the Pacha's tent without any special guard, but loose and free of his person, and able to look about him in the camp; but when, by help of God, the Turks being repulsed broke up their Camp, the Pacha took the Count with him the first day's march, but in the morning put another Turkish robe of velvet on him over the former, and added a present of a hundred aspers, and also a cavalry prisoner whom the Count knew and had begged for, and caused them to be honourably attended and passed safe, so that on the following day they reached Vienna, where the Count was honourably received by the princes, counts, gentlemen and officers there present."

Such instances of chivalrous behaviour are not at all rare, but to balance the picture one must remember the appalling excesses of which the Turks were sometimes guilty. At this same siege of Vienna the *azabs* and *akinjis* ravished and pillaged right into Styria, burning villages by the score and blotting out every trace of life over large areas. Worst of all was the scene when the Turks realized that it was beyond their power to take Vienna, and the order was given to break up camp. The troops set fire to their stores and encampment and when the blaze under the city walls was at its height a large number of the prisoners in the camp were thrown alive on the flames in full view of the Viennese populace. It is only fair to say that Suleyman himself did not sanction, even if he failed to prevent, this atrocious act.

Selim II, whom we left at Adrianople, confronting the bedizened corpse of his father, was the first of a series of dissolute sultans, but he continued Suleyman's agressive policy during the short eight years of his reign. The centre of his attacks shifted, however, east and west, against the Venetians on one side and the Don Cossacks on the other. He won Cyprus and lost the battle of Lepanto. In one very important respect he broke with the Turkish traditions. From the earliest tribal days the Ottoman sultans had led their troops in battle, and Suleyman the Magnificent had commanded in person on all his campaigns. Selim was the first exception : he sent his Grand Vizir into the field at the head of his armies and employed his own time in ignoble pursuits at home.

This altered custom was typical of the change which had come over Turkey and was the first milestone on the steep descent down which the country was soon to plunge. Five models of ineptitude succeeded Selim— Murad III, whose reign included two of the events which find a place in this book, namely the adventures of Dallam, the organ-builder, and the dreadful experiences of the young Baron Wratislaw; Mohammed III; Ahmed I whose absurd fulminations against the "Princes of Christendom" have already been quoted, and who occupied the seraglio at the time of Sandys' visit; the gentle imbecile Mustapha I and finally Osman II who figures in the battle with the Poles at Chocim which is described in the diary of an eye-witness in chapter IX.

War with the Holy Roman Empire broke out again under Murad III, but the Janissaries who by now were embarking on their wild career of bloodshed and anarchy no longer maintained their invincibility and the Turkish armies lost more than they gained in the struggle. Murad being dead, Mohammed was forced by a handful of patriots to quit for a moment the pleasures of the seraglio and take the field at the head of the army. The sight of their Sultan leading them to battle as in the good old days revived the spirit of the troops to such a degree that they inflicted a crushing defeat on the Austrians at the battle of Cerestes. The peace which ensued ended the Hungarian wars for twenty years to come. Turkey kept most of her gains in Europe but it was a significant sign of the times that the Sultan for the first time in history treated with Christian monarchs as *his own equals* and not as merely the " brothers " of his Vizir.

During the next fifty years the balance between Turkey and Christendom remained at a standstill. It was really the pause of the tide before it changed to the ebb, and though the Turkish terror persisted for a time among Christian peoples, it is clear enough that the Turks had by now missed their chance to become a great civilization and were doomed to give way before the march of progress in Europe. Internally the rot was eating away the careful fabric built up by Suleyman. Three successive sultans ascended the throne at the ages respectively of 14, 11, and 7, and even those others who at least were grown men when they came to power had passed their whole previous life imprisoned in the seraglio in special quarters, known as "the cage."

Murad IV, whose iron discipline and ruthless "efficiency" appear in the narrative of Henry Blunt, formed a break in the line of worthless voluptuaries. He at least was a man of decision and action. The country was soaked in corruption and anarchy when he mounted the throne ; he treated its ills with a simple panacea ; every officer and every official who incurred his slightest suspicion of unloyal or dishonest behaviour lost his head in a trice, while a ferocious massacre of their leaders quelled the unruly Janissaries from the start. Murad, however, had little contact with Europe but was chiefly occupied in regaining from Persia what Shah Abbas the Great had won from his predecessor.

Persia and Turkey have clashed throughout history but their sternest struggles were in Murad's reign, when the Turks took Erivan and recovered possession of Bagdad which they held till the day when British troops followed General Maude through its gates.

Murad was succeeded by the worst of all the bad sultans, Ibrahim. Jewelled coaches, rare furs and Georgian ladies were the only objects of his existence and the little time he spared from them he devoted to the persecution of his *rayahs*. Regicide for once was justified when the Janissaries rose and killed him. His only interest for us is that, in revenge for the capture by a Venetian sea-captain of one of his sultanas travelling to Mecca, he started the Cretan war and the siege of Candia whither Monsieur de la Feuillade led his forlorn hope as recorded in chapter XIII.

Ibrahim was followed by Mohammed IV who, though by no means great in himself, had the sense to choose a great man as Vizir. This man was Mohammed Kiuprulu, an Albanian by birth who started life as a palace cook, rose to be Vali and at the age of seventy was offered the Grand Vizirate. He took it on condition that the Sultan should give him absolute powers and at once began a thorough purging of the Turkish system. His methods were similar to those of Murad IV, and in the five years of his Vizirate he was credited with no less than 36,000 capital executions.

His son Ahmed who followed him led a large army into Hungary against the great Count Montecuculi. The Thirty Years' War had taught Europe new methods in military science and put European armies ahead of the conservative Turks, who, for instance, kept to their sabres and failed to realize the superior possibilities of the pike as an infantry weapon. Nor could all the Kiuprulus' efforts at regeneration cope with the indiscipline and corruption which had rooted themselves in the nation. The consequence was that the great Imperialist general utterly routed a Turkish force four times his own in numbers and took all their artillery at the battle of St Gotthard. Ahmed retrieved the disaster to a great extent by the astuteness he showed in the subsequent treaty which left Turkey suzerain over Transylvania. He also won the Ukraine from John Sobiesky, the chivalrous King of Poland, who was destined fifteen years later to be the instrument of Europe's liberation from the secular Turkish menace.

When Ahmed died in 1676 his immediate successor was not, unhappily for Turkey, another of the same family. Sultan Mohammed chose instead a man who was noted throughout the country for boundless greed and ambition. He was known as Black Mustafa and he is believed to have aimed at advancing the boundaries of Turkey to the Rhine and making himself Viceroy of a huge province extending thither from the Danube. With some such plan in view he urged the Sultan to war with Austria. The situation in Hungary was most propitious for the Turkish invasion as the country was racked with internecine strife. The Hungarians had lost all patience with the tyranny of the Emperor and his ruthless measures to crush the Protestants, and had formed a secret league against the Austrians. The insurgents invited the help of the Sultan who responded only too readily and assembled the whole Turkish army for an attack on Vienna. In chapter XII we have the account of a Venetian dragoman who tells of the preparations for the great campaign, the assembling and the march northward of the huge Turkish army numbering nearly half-a-million men and of the desperate scenes which occurred when they returned later in rout and confusion. Vienna was saved by the unexpected accession of the Poles to the Austrian cause and the brilliant and successful onslaught which their King Sobiesky made at the eleventh hour on the beleaguering Turkish army. An important contributory cause, however, was the inordinate greed of Black Mustafa whose claim to keep for himself all the money which might be taken from the city so disgusted his men that they lost heart in the fight. A proof of his extraordinary taste for fantastic luxury is supplied in a letter which Sobiesky wrote to his Queen describing Mustafa's camp as it was found when the Austrian troops entered it.

He mentions the Vizir's charger discovered standing at the door of the tent so weighed down with its heavy caparisons including stirrups of solid gold as to be useless for flight, the tent itself full of carpets and furs, jewelled arms and quivers studded with rubies and pearls and the enormous private camp containing not only fountains and baths, but even (*mirabile dictu*) a rabbit-warren and a small menagerie. A parrot took wing and foiled the pursuit of the Austrian soldiers and, strangest of all, a pet ostrich was found which had been beheaded by Mustafa's own sword to prevent its falling into Christian hands. A trophy of special interest was a large wooden cross which had regularly been set up in the Turkish camp for the mass celebrations of Contacuzenos, the Prince of Wallachia, the Sultan's Christian vassal.

Mustafa paid the price of his failure with his life, meeting the messenger with the bow string ere ever he reached the shores of the Bosphorus. His head was carried to be shown to the Sultan who ordered that it should be taken to Belgrade and deposited there in a mosque. When the Turks lost Belgrade they left the grisly relic behind and it found its way to Vienna where, for all that I know to the contrary, it still lies in the city arsenal.

The victory of the Christian arms was set off by the appalling depredations of the Turkish troops. A contemporary Austrian record mentions that 4092 villages in the district of Vienna were burnt, and gives the following table of prisoners carried off into Turkish captivity :

Old men	6,000
Women	11,215
Unmarried women, 26 years of age at the oldest, of whom 204 were noble ...	14,922
Children, boys and girls, the oldest between 4 and 5 years of age...	26,093
Total	57,220 (*sic*)

The colossal *débâcle* at Vienna was followed by a series of further disasters including the loss of Buda-Pesth, which had then been Turkish for 145 years, and the occupation by the Venetians of a large part of Greece. Two more Kiuprulus held the post of Vizir, the latter of whom, in the reign of Mustafa II, concluded the treaty of Carlowitz.

On this famous occasion the Turks entered the conference chamber possessing nearly a quarter of Europe, if Russia be excluded; they emerged with the loss of all Hungary except the Banat, half of Greece, the southern portion of Poland and a great stretch of the north coast of the Black Sea, to which Russia now descended for the first time. But the treaty of Carlowitz was signed in the last year of the seventeenth century and we have already overshot the end of the period with which we are immediately concerned.

CHAPTER II

THE OLD SERAGLIO AND THE ADVENTURES OF AN ORGAN-BUILDER

No city on the earth has, I suppose, had such encomiums lavished upon it by literary travellers as Constantinople.

One names it "the Mistress of two Continents," another "the Navel of the World" and all vie together in enthusiastic praises of its natural beauties. The limit of absurd hyperbole is reached by an early French writer—whose name I forget—when he solemnly affirms that not only do all the birds of the air flock to the neighbouring shores to revel in its charms, but that the very oysters of the Bosphorus may be seen leaping high above the waves to catch a glimpse of its unrivalled glories.

A captious critic might possibly observe that although the Bosphorus furnishes the epicure with as great a variety of piscatorial delicacies as any waters in the world, these do not include oysters, and further that the birds which are to be seen in such numbers flitting to and fro along its shores, so far from being joyful visitants, are of a particularly mournful species known locally as the "souls of the damned" and reputed to embody the spirits of drowned miscreants.

We can, however, easily forgive the old writer's pretty bit of extravagance, for the subject which inspired it has, in truth, hardly an equal in the world. Its seven hills crowned with minarets and mosques, its graceful slopes falling away to the water's edge, its many cypress groves and the sparkling girdle which the Marmora and Golden Horn throw three-parts around it form a truly exquisite *ensemble*.

Such a spot is, as Sandys felicitously puts it, a seat of sovereignty, "by destinie appointed and by nature seal'd"; in proof of which the city has never ceased to harbour an Emperor for the last seventeen centuries.

The Byzantine emperors had their marble and porphyry palaces high up on the hill, but the Ottoman Sultans built theirs down by the water's edge on a small promontory jutting into the Sea of Marmora. Here a vast rambling conglomeration of courtyards and kiosks set among woods and gardens and surrounded by a formidable wall three miles in circumference gave them complete seclusion from the vulgar gaze of the populace. Sandys during his visit to Constantinople in 1610 gained admittance to the Serai which he describes as follows: "The space within comprehendeth goodly groves of cypresses intermixed with plaines, delicate gardens, artificell fountaines, all varietie of fruit trees and what not rare; luxury being the steward and the treasure inexhaustible. The proud Pallace of the Tyrant doth open to the South, having a loftie gate-house ingraven with Arabick characters set forth with gold and azure all on white marble. This leadeth into a spacious court 300 yardes long and about half as wide, on the left hand whereof stands the round of an ancient Chappell containing the armes that were taken from the Graecians in the subversion of the Citie, and at the farre end of this court a second gate hung with shields and cymitars doth lead into another full of tall cypress trees. The

SERAGLIO POINT

From Grelot's *Voyage de Constantinople*, 1680

Cloysters about it are leaded above and paved with stone, the roof supported with columnes of marble having copper chapters and bases.   On the left hand the Divan is kept where the Bassas of the Porte do administer justice, and on that side confined with humble buildings; beyond which court there is a stretch of kitchens.   On the left is a stable large enough for 500 horses.   Out of this second court there is a passage with a third not by Christians ordinarily to be entered, surrounded with the royal buildings which, though perhaps they come short of the Italian for contrivement and finenesse yet not in costly curiousnesse.   Between the East wall and the water a sort of terrible Ordnance are planted which threaten destruction to such as by sea shall attempt a violent entrie.   Without, on the North side stands the Sultan's Cabinet in form of a summer house, having a private passage of waxed linen from his seraglio where he often solaceth himself with the various objects of his harem and from thence takes barge to passe unto the delight-fulle places of adjoyning Asia."

These "delicate gardens" with their well kept parterres of roses, tulips and ranunculus are mentioned with admiration by most writers on Constantinople. Foreign travellers however who succeeded in bribing their way past the Guardians of the Gate, were apt to find their visits spiced with a good bit of excitement. Instant decapitation was at least a possible result of meeting with the palace eunuchs when they were escorting the harem ladies through the grounds, and one writer tells how he and several Turks who were with him, finding themselves suddenly face to face with a fair, but well-guarded sultana, only escaped with their lives by imitating the gardeners in *Alice in Wonderland* when the Red Queen made her appearance, and throwing themselves flat on their faces till the lady and her companions had passed.

All the Sultan's gardens were in the charge of the Head Gardener, the *Bostanji Bashi*, who had ten thousand under-gardeners beneath him. The functions of this dignitary extended far beyond the cultivation of his flower beds; indeed he ranked as one of the highest officers of State, being more or less in the position of a Lord High Chamberlain. There are even several instances in Ottoman history of the Head Gardener marrying the Sultan's daughter. The enormous number of his underlings is an example of the lavish way in which the imperial household was staffed. An Italian book, written in 1470, gives the following table showing the pay-roll:

"Cooks	50
Sweet-makers	30
Carpet layers	60
Door keepers	250
Grooms	150
Kennelmen	2000
Ditto for pet-dogs	600
Falconers	200"

These figures show the number of the personnel at a period—only fifty years after the conquest of Constantinople—when the extravagance of the court was very far short of reaching the scale it did under succeeding sultans, and a century later the numbers were certainly many times greater.

Among the most peculiar features of the Turkish court was the method of recruiting and training the court officials. The janissaries, whom I shall have occasion to describe in greater detail when dealing with the army, were primarily intended to furnish fighting men, but a certain proportion of them were educated for the public services and the Sultan's own employ. They were the sons of Christian *rayahs* ravished from their homes at the age of ten under the cruel system of human tithe which the Turks initiated at an early date, and were trained for their vocation in life in a special college standing within the grounds of the imperial palace.

The early career of one of these lads, who were known as *ich-oghlans* or "house boys," was very far from enviable. After being initiated into the Moslem faith he was put into the college and started on a course of probationary training of the most rigorous nature conceivable. He was bastinadoed for the slightest fault and systematically bullied by the ill-tempered eunuchs who had charge of the pupils. During their six years novitiate the probationers never once left the confines of the palace but spent their time acquiring a general education designed to inculcate good manners, accuracy and honesty. Humility was the keynote of the system and—to borrow from M. Tournefort's book of Turkish travels—the inmates of the college were "bred in exemplary modesty and taught above all to remain silent, keep their eyes lowered and their arms folded across their breasts." This last describes the typical attitude assumed at all times by the janissaries when in the presence of their superiors.

At the end of the first period the pupils entered upon a second course or, to use the Turkish phrase, into the second "Chamber," where they studied Turkish, Arabic and Persian literature and had instructors to teach them dart-throwing, pike and lance drill and equitation. Four more years brought them to the third and last Chamber where they acquired the gentler arts of music, needlework and embroidery, arrow-splicing, hair-dressing and manicure, valeting and the care and treatment of birds and pet dogs. In this Chamber they were allowed more freedom, but in the lower two they were kept under the sternest discipline and could not even talk together except at certain fixed times of the day.

Only a fraction of the boys who entered at the bottom completed the whole course. Many were eliminated after the first Chamber and passed straight into the ranks of the fighting janissaries. Of those who reached the middle Chamber some would be allotted to mediocre posts without further training, becoming for instance clerks in the Treasury or servers in the palace laboratory, where among other duties they had to mix the Sultan's liquors and cordials.

Only aspirants to the higher offices continued into the third Chamber—barely one-tenth of each batch. Its members were a privileged class and discarded the plain clothes of the novice for a sumptuous dress of satin brocade or cloth of gold. When proficient in the accomplishments taught in that Chamber, they were appointed to various posts in the Sultan's personal suite, such as his sword-bearer, stirrup-knight, master of the wardrobe, barber and manicurist, turban-valet or keeper of the pet dogs. A few chosen youths acted as pages. We are told that Suleyman I had six of these, two of whom were always with him both by day or night. Every morning a page filled two purses, one with a thousand silver aspers, the other with twenty ducats of gold, and

strapped them to his master's waist. With this fund
Suleyman met the current needs of the day, and whatever was left over at night became the perquisite of the
lucky page who undressed him. While he was awake
the two lads waited at his side, and when he slept they
stood with torches at the head and foot of his bed.

By a custom, which at first sight seems more typical
of a Gilbertian play than of real life, the ministers of
state and high functionaries of the empire were commonly
selected from among these royal lackeys and it was no
unusual thing for a favourite *ich-oghlan* to leave his duties
as parer of the Sultan's nails for the governorship of a
province. In point of fact, though, the long and very
liberal course of education which these Christian boys
went through before they graduated from the janissaries'
college probably made them fitter candidates for public
posts than any Turks in the empire, and the system
was certainly no worse than that which obtained in European countries. The difference in systems illustrates,
by the way, a peculiar feature of Turkish society—the
entire absence of the "hereditary principle." In Turkey
a great man could bequeath to his son neither title nor
honours so that he had no better claim to position
and rank than the son of a beggar. Most of the Grand
Vizirs rose from the ranks and had begun life as
porters or cowherds or in some other equally lowly
state of life, and a pasha's "tails" were well within the
reach of even a black eunuch. The sultanate itself did
not descend by right from father to son but passed on
a sultan's death to the *doyen* of the royal family, though
it is true that the golden rule of killing off all possible
rivals left little distinction in effect between the Turkish
system and the commoner one of primogeniture.

But to return to the subject from which we have wandered, the *ich-oghlans* whom I have just described had humbler brethren known as *ajami oghlans*. This class was drawn from the same source and reared on the same general principles, but their training was shorter and confined to bodily exercises; they lived also in meaner quarters, in sheds along the shore and were clad—like Christ's Hospital boys—in a dress of dark blue and yellow.

When they left school they were employed in subordinate posts as *chaoushes*, *capujis*, gardeners, cooks, grooms, huntsmen etc., or, in the case of a favoured few, as archers of the guard or rowers in the Sultan's caïque. The *capujis*, or door-keepers, who were a not unimportant class, provided a guard of 15 men at each door of the Seraglio, where they levied heavy blackmail on foreign ambassadors visiting the Porte. The *chaoushes* were primarily footmen and couriers (the *Chaoush Bashi* was incidentally Grand Master of Ceremonies), but their occupations were numerous and varied and they acted generally as men-of-all-trades. Not the least uncommon of their multifarious duties was to travel under the Sultan's orders to the province of an objectionable Pasha and return with his head (pickled) in a bag.

This mention of the executioner's profession brings us to the palace mutes, the high priests of that gentle art. Highly placed victims, such as Vizirs who had fallen from favour, were alone honoured with their attentions. The technique of that peculiarly Turkish institution the bowstring was highly developed at the Porte and in the hands of a skillful operator the most taciturn subjects could be made to part with their innermost secrets before the fatal twist. The process of persuading a dumb man to speak doubtless held special attractions for the tongue-tied executioner himself!

Much more could be added about the Sultan's court and its surroundings, but these abstract descriptions are apt to pall and the reader will doutless be better pleased to pass on at once to the narrative of an Englishman who was himself an actor in the scenes he describes. Master Thomas Dallam is our man—an organ-builder in Queen Elizabeth's reign. How a gentleman of his craft should, in the pursuance of his profession, find himself in the awesome presence of the "Grand Turke" himself would certainly seem a mystery. Let me solve it by explaining the circumstances. At a certain point in her struggle with Philip, Elizabeth harboured the notion of a Turkish alliance. The Ottoman fleet, though well past its prime, could do much to embarrass the Spaniards, and the Queen went so far as to appeal to Mohammed III for assistance in the name of religion, on the grounds that Moslem and Protestant were united in their hatred of "image-worshippers." She thought well, however, to back up the appeal with a more material argument and so arranged with the Levant Company—then a close corporation for trading with Turkey—for the purchase and despatch to Constantinople of a gift to the Sultan in the form of an organ.

Dallam, who had just finished the erection of the organ in Kings' College, Cambridge, was entrusted with the work and in the year 1599 the organ was completed (it was the Levant Company, one need hardly mention, who had to pay for it!) and, having been packed in sections, was shipped together with Dallam to Constantinople.

The room in the Seraglio which was set aside for

the erection of the instrument was a beautiful kiosk with walls of porphyry topped by a course of lattice work fitted with awnings to moderate the heat and a fish pond in the centre with silk carpets all round. It had—so Dallam at any rate was made to believe—been specially constructed as a theatre for the strangling of members of the royal family, for whose comfort in their last moments these pleasant features were considerately provided. Here in the course of a week or two Dallam reconstructed his organ and a day was fixed for the Sultan to come and hear it play. The instrument had an automatic arrangement by which it could be made to play like a musical box and Dallam, after setting the clockwork to go off at the appropriate moment, was made to wait outside. The Sultan arrived and the organ performed its tricks; first it struck twenty-two times, then followed a chime of sixteen bells, after which it played a four-part song and, as a grand finale, two figures with silver trumpets lifted them to their lips and played a fanfare, while a nestful of wooden blackbirds and thrushes set in a holly bush at the top of the machine flapped their wings and sang a chorus. This pyrotechnic display greatly pleased Mohammed, and Dallam was summoned into his presence. Let him from this point take up the narrative himself:

"When I came within the Dore that which I did see was verrie wonderful unto me. I came in direcktly upon the Grand Sinyori's ryghte hande, but he would not turne his head to louke upon me. He satt in greate state, yeate the sighte of him was nothinge in Comparison of the traine which stoode behind him and made me almost to thinke that I was in another worlde. I stood dazlinge my eyes with loukinge upon his

people, the which was 4 hundrethe persons in number.
200 weare his principall padgis appareled in ritche clothe
of goulde made in gownes to the midlegge, upon their
heades litle caps; greate peeces of silke abowte their
wastes; upon their legges reade Cordovan buskins.
Theire heades weare all shaven savinge that behind
their eares did hange a locke of hare like a squirel's
taile. They weare very proper men and Christian born.

"The third hundred were Dum men who could
neither heare nor speake and they likewise in riche
clothe of golde but theire caps weare of violet velvett,
the crowne of them made like a lether bottell, the brims
divided into 5 peaked corners. Some had hawkes on
theire fistes.

"The fourth hundred weare all dwarffes, big-bodied
men but very low of stature; everyone did weare a
simmetare by his side.

"When I had stode nearly $\frac{1}{4}$ of an houre behouldinge
this wonderful syghte I hearde the Grand Sinyori speake
unto the Cappagan (viz. Capuji) who then came to me
and touke my cloake from aboute me and layed it downe
upon the carpetes and bid me go playe on the organ;
but I refused because the Grande Sinyori satt so neare
that I coulde not come at the place and muste needes
turne my backe towards him and touche his knee with
my britchis, which no man in paine of deathe myght
doo save only the Cappagan.

"So he smyled and let me stande a litle. Then the
Grand Sinyori spoake again and the Cappagan with a
merrie countenance bid me go with goode curridge and
thruste me on.

"When I came verrie neare the Grand Sinyori I
bowed my heade as low as my knee and turned my

backe righte tow him. He satt so righte behind me
that he could not see what I did; Therfor he stoode
up and the Cappagan removed his chaire to one side
wher he myghte see my handes, but in his risinge from
his chaire he gave me a thruste forwardes and I thought
he had bene drawinge his sorde to cut off my heade.

"I stood thar playinge suche things as I could untill the cloke strouke. Then I went close to the Grande
Sinyori againe and bowed myself and wente backwardes
to my Cloake. When the Company saw me theye
seemed to be glad and laughed. Then the Grande
Sinyori put his hande behind him full of goulde which
the Cappagan receved and brought unto me fortie and
five peeces and then was I put out againe wheare I
came in beinge not a litle joyfull of my good suckses."

Left to the tender mercies of the Turks, the organ,
needless to relate, soon went out of order and Dallam
was called in again to repair it. While at work on the
repairs he made friends with some of the *ajami oghlans*,
who did their best to persuade him to turn Turk and
stay at Constantinople, in which case "they toulde me
the Grand Sinyori would give me two wyfes of the
beste I coulde chuse myselfe in cittie or countrie." To
escape their blandishments Dallam, who actually was
a bachelor, had to invent a wife and family at home in
England to whom, he said, the bonds of natural affection
forced him to return.

One day his palace friends took Dallam all round
the palace. They came in the course of their tour to
a blank wall with a small iron grille in it which they
told him to look through, though they would not themselves go near. On looking he saw thirty or forty persons playing at ball. "At the firste syghte of them I

TURKISH LADY IN INDOOR DRESS
From George Sandys' *Travels*, 1632

thoughte they had bene yonge men, but when I saw
the hair of theire heades hange doone on their backes
platted with a tasle of small pearles and by other plaine
tokens I did know them to be women and verrie prettie
ones in deede.

"They wore a litle capp which did but cover the
crowne of the heade, faire chaines of pearls and juels in
their ears, coats like a souldier's mandilyon some of red
sattan and som of blew, britchis of fine clothe made of
coton woll as whyte as snow and as fine as lawne. Som
did weare fine cordovan buskins and som had their leges
naked with a goulden ring on the smale of her legg, on
her foute a panttoble 4 or 5 inches hie. I stoode so long
loukinge upon them that he which had brought me began to be verrie angrie with me and made a wrye mouthe
and stamped with his foute to make me give over
loukinge ; the which I was verrie lothe to dow, for the
sighte did please me wondrous well."

He subsequently learnt that he had been watching
the ladies of the Sultan's own harem, an offence only to
be expiated by instant death or worse.

One last adventure befell our organ-builder before
he left Constantinople. He had nearly completed the
repair of the organ but still had some of the pipes spread
on the floor of the kiosk when his Turkish assistants
suddenly and without any explanation bolted. "By
chance," he writes, "I called to my drugaman and asked
him the cause. He said the Grande Sinyori and his
conquebines weare cominge and we must be gone in
paine of deathe. Then they all ran away and lefte me
behinde and before I gott out of the house they had run
over the greene quit out of the gate and I ran as fast
as my leges would carrie me after and 4 neagers or

blackamoors came runninge towards me with their semetars drawne; if they coulde have catchte me they would have hewed me all in peecis. When I cam to the wickett there stood a greate number of jemoglans prayinge that I mite escape the handes of those runninge wolves and when I was got out of the gate they were verrie juyfull that I had so well escaped."

Having accompanied Dallam so far, let us see him safe home again to his native town. He fell seriously ill after his fright from the eunuchs with the "semetars" and his boat had to sail from the Golden Horn without him. He recovered sufficiently to follow a few weeks after in another English merchantman and though in a parlous state during most of the voyage was almost restored to health when at length they reached England. Full of satisfaction at having faithfully accomplished the task on which he had set out months before, he welcomed the sight of the English coast. "Then," he concludes, "we wente ashore at Dover and our trompetes soundinge all the waye before us into the towne where we made ourselves as merrie as could. So at tow of the Clocke we touke poste horse to Canterburie and from thence to Rochester that nyghte and the nexte day to London."

CHAPTER III

THE SULTAN'S ARMIES

The Sultan's armies comprised five principal branches—first and foremost the janissaries, then the feudal troops, the *spahis* and *piadés*, thirdly the artillery, fourthly the irregular troops, *azabs*, *akinjis* and the rest, and lastly the Tartar auxiliaries.

All of them are interesting and picturesque, but none so much as the janissaries, that wonderful corps of which an eminent writer has said that "it was one of the most remarkable bodies the world has ever seen, and goes far to explain the character of the early Ottoman Empire—that wild brilliancy and vigour in which no ordinary ideas of humanity, morality or economy find a place."

Tradition places the foundation of the corps in the reign of Sultan Orkhan, who succeeded Sultan Osman (founder of the Ottoman nation) and flourished 200 years before the capture of Constantinople.

Several causes combined to bring it to birth. The Ottomans were hopelessly unable—both from their lack of assimilative power and the rapidity of their progress—to digest their conquests in Europe and Asia, and the numbers and strength of their subject populations became a serious problem. Conversion to Islam was an obvious remedy and in seeking methods of encouraging this they hit on the janissary system. It was a brilliant solution from their own point of view, for it killed three birds at least with a single stone. It formed a deadly inducement to Christian parents to abandon their faith for the sake of their children; where this failed, it lessened the danger from the Christian element by removing the pick of each generation, and it provided ideal material for the Turkish armies.

Its invention is credited by Turkish historians to one "Black Khalil," the Vizir of Sultan Orkhan, who suggested to his master that he should levy an annual tribute of one thousand children, selected at discretion, from the Christians under his power. The scheme was adopted and the boys were reft from their homes with the same ruthlessness as the victims of the Minotaur, and forcibly initiated, by the customary rites, into Islam. The initiation was performed by a notable holy man, Hajji Bektash (founder of the Bektashi order of Dervishes which still flourishes in Turkey), who, we are told, blessed the neophytes by stretching his flowing sleeve above the head of their leader lying prostrate before him on the ground and pronouncing the following words: "Let these youths be called the Yeni Cheri (meaning the 'New Armies' and corrupted by European lips to 'Janissaries'); let their countenance ever be bright, their hands victorious and their swords clean, and whithersoever they go, may they return always with a white face!" The corps adopted the peculiar mystic tenets taught by the Hajji and for centuries after preserved the memory of their baptismal day by wearing a piece of stuff, shaped like a miniature sleeve, attached to the peak of their caps.

The janissaries were forbidden to marry, and passed their lives under a system of military discipline of the sternest imaginable nature. To quote from Sir Charles

A JANISSARY

From Nicolay's *Pérégrinations faictes en la Turquie*, 1577

Eliot, "they were thus a military religious order composed of men selected for physical and mental excellence, divorced more completely than any monk from all worldly ties of birth, marriage or profession, and encouraged to give their vigour full and unscrupulous play subject to no law save that of unquestioning obedience to their superior officers." The system produced, indeed, a *corps d'élite* of incomparable fighters, and any fears which their founders may have entertained as to the standard of loyalty to be looked for from a body of forced converts were speedily dispelled when the young converts proved themselves capable of even fiercer acts of tyranny and oppression towards their own Christian relations than the natural-born sons of the Prophet. In this way the Turks organized the first regular standing army which Europe had known since Roman times, and developed it steadily until, by the time of Suleyman I, the corps reached a strength of 40,000.

We have already, in the first chapter of this book, had a glimpse of the embryo janissary during his period of training in the seraglio. On leaving school he was posted to an *orta* or company, in which he usually remained for the rest of his life. This was a self-contained unit organized on such communistic lines as could not fail to win the approbation of the most uncompromising modern bolshevik. All pay and expenses were pooled, and contributions were levied from each member of the company to form a common purse which provided pensions for the sick and funds for general purposes. The principle of equality was carried so far that when issues of stores or equipment took place the distribution was made at night to prevent any possibility of favouritism. One writer asserts, though one hesitates to believe it,

that even the armour captured from Christian troops
(the Turks made none themselves and only used what
they obtained in this manner) was deliberately parcelled
out at haphazard, so that a janissary in the ranks could
often be seen wearing an assortment of ill-fitting pieces,
the original property of half-a-dozen Christians of vary-
ing girth and stature.   The supreme instance of the
democratic foundation of the corps lay in the fact that
the Sultan, though like the Czar he was "father" to
every janissary, himself held the rank of a common
private and drew his weekly pay accordingly.

A curious feature among the janissaries was the
regimental "stew-pot."   These great cauldrons played
a vital part in the life of the regiment; they were vene-
rated as we venerate a regiment's colours, and were
carried at the head of the column on all occasions, while
a regiment which lost its cauldron in battle was disgraced eternally.   The cooks held a proud and important
position in the corps and the prestige of the kitchen may
be gauged by the strange title given to company commanders, namely *chorbaji* or "soup-man."

The janissary's hierarchy was a simple one.   At the
head was the Agha of the corps, who was accounted the
third greatest man in the Empire.   Under him were the
commanders of *buluks* and *jema'ats* (the latter including
the cavalry), distinguishable from each other only by the
colour of their boots, red and yellow respectively.   These
units were subdivided into the *ortas* mentioned above,
each of which was distinguished by an individual crest,
such as for instance an anchor, embroidered on its standard, painted above the barracks and frequently tattooed
on the persons of its members.   The janissaries were divided also into various 'arms', archers (*sulaks*), fusiliers

So ◦ _Aga Capitaine general des Ianiſſaires._

THE *AGHA* OF THE JANISSARIES

From Nicolay's *Pérégrinations faictes en la Turquie,* 1577

(*tufankjis*), gunners (*topjis*), camelry etc, besides non-combatant branches such as the foresters.

Side by side with the spirit of democracy there existed an iron discipline within the corps. On the first occasion that a batch of new janissaries entered the palace they filed past the Agha each holding on to the coat-tails of the man in front. The Agha gave every one as he passed a hearty smack in the face and a twitch of the ears and received in return a reverential salute from the victim as a token of loyal obedience.

Absolute obedience to his superiors was indeed the first article of the janissary's charter which consisted—like another famous document—of fourteen points. The remaining thirteen were: (2) perfect harmony within the corps, (3) abstention from all things unbefitting a brave man, (4) adherence to the precepts of Hajji Bektash, (5) right to be recruited only in the established way, (6) in the case of men condemned to death for any misdeed, privilege of private execution by night and of a *coup de canon* at the moment when the body was thrown into the sea, (7) immunity from punishment by anyone except officers of the corps, (8) promotion by seniority, (9) pension for old age, (10) obligation to shave the chin, (11) celibacy, (12) prohibition to sleep outside barracks or (13) to follow a trade, (14) liability in peace time to take part in manoeuvres from June to November.

The janissary's uniform was of dark blue cloth, plainly cut and comparatively free from ornamentation. Its simplicity was compensated for by the elaborate magnificence of their headdress. This consisted of a white felt hat shaped after the fashion affected by Marlborough's Grenadiers, richly embroidered round the base

and resolving itself behind into the sleeve-like append-
age which commemorated their religious initiation; to
the front was attached a gilt sheath encrusted with bastard stones and into this was stuck—if the wearer was
a veteran soldier—a prodigious Bird-of-Paradise plume
which fell in a magnificent curve down his back and
reached nearly to the level of his knees. When stationed
at Constantinople the janissaries carried silver-tipped
batons some six feet long with which they performed
summary execution on anyone found breaking the laws.
A feature which distinguished them from the bearded
Turks was their shaven chins. This was supposed to
impart a fierceness of expression unattainable by the
wearer of a beard, and the effect was further enhanced
by the cultivation of long and ferocious moustaches.

Of the functions of the janissaries one of the chief
was to police the country, and under the great Sultans
they were such efficient guardians of the peace that
travellers reported the roads in Turkey to be as safe or
safer than in any Christian country. Especially in the
reign of Murad IV—the most bloodthirsty monster who
ever donned the cloak and mantle of Osman—the punishment of crime was so drastic and so sure that people
said, as in days of Charlemagne, that a woman could
carry a basket of jewels in safety from one end of the
empire to the other.

A foreigner of distinction, on entering the Turkish
dominions, was given a small bodyguard of janissaries
(a custom which survived until the beginning of the
recent war in the privilege accorded to diplomatic
and consular representatives to have a fixed number of
armed *cavasses* attached to their persons), and a delightful sketch of one of these guards has come down to us

in the memoirs of an old ambassador to the Porte, written in the middle of the sixteenth century. "The Janizaries," he says, "came to me by couples. When they were admitted into my dining-room they bowed their heads and made obeisance, and presently they ran hastily to me and touched either my garment or my hand, as if they would have kissed it; and then forced upon me a bundle or nosegay of narcissuses, and presently retired backwards with equal speed to the door, that so they might not turn their backs on me, for that is accounted undecent by the rules of their order. At the door they bowed their heads again and wishing me all happiness, departed. The truth is, unless I had been told before they were Janizaries, I should have thought them to be some kind of Turkish monks, or Fellows of some College or other amongst them; yet these are the Janizaries that carry such terror with them wheresoever they go."

As time went on the original strictness of the order became relaxed, and when celibacy ceased to be enforced the old method of recruiting from among the children of the Christian *raiahs* gave way to the custom of enlisting the sons of ex-janissaries. In these later days, under a series of weak and dissolute Sultans, the janissaries followed in the footsteps of the Turkish Guards of the Baghdad Caliphs and the Mamelukes in Egypt though they never, like these, actually usurped the throne itself. Even in Suleyman's time the janissaries extorted higher pay by threats of mutiny or worse, and in the reigns of the next few Sultans their power grew to such an extent that no Vizir could be appointed without their sanction. By the middle of the seventeenth century they had become absolute arbiters of the Sultan's fate and had been guilty three times over of the supreme sacrilege of assassinating their own Caliph, besides deposing three others. Affairs by the end of the century had reached such a pass that an English traveller of the period writes of them, "the mortallest corruption of this Order hath set in of late yeares; knowing their owne strength and growne saucy with familiarity at Court they have proceeded to such insolency as hath flesh'd them in the blood of their Sovereigns and have learnt that damnable Secret of making and unmaking their King at their pleasure whereby the Foundation of all Monarchy, that is the due awe towards the Blood Royall, is so irreparably decayed in them that, like the lost State of Innocence, it can never be restored."

They had a peculiar method of their own for expressing their discontent with the Government of the moment. When the huge bowls of rice which formed their daily rations were set out in the seraglio courtyard (as is described by the Italian diplomat from whose diary I quote in chapter IV), the *Orta Bashıs*, instead of quietly carrying them to their messes, turned them upside down on the ground. This was a pretty sure omen of riot and bloodshed and woe betide the reigning Sultan when it happened. Not till early in the nineteenth century did Turkey free herself from the incubus of these insolent tyrants, when that passionate reformer Mahmud II abolished the corps for good and all by the simple expedient of a wholesale massacre.

The *spahis* and *piadés*, who, unlike the janissaries, were trueborn Turks, originated under much the same system as our own feudal troops. The Sultans, as they extended their conquests in Europe, parcelled out a large proportion of the conquered land into fiefs, or *timars*, which they gave to their followers in recognition of special services in the field. The "timariot' held his land on much the same terms as a Norman baron, being bound to accompany his liege-lord whenever he went to war, and to bring with him a quota of armed retainers proportionate to the size of his holding.

The military equipment of a *spahi* riding to the wars has been detailed by an old English writer, whose description reminds one of nothing so much as John Tenniel's picture of the Red Knight. It reads as follows:—

"First the girdle stuck with three or four pistols, then on each side a knife as long as a man's arm with another of a foot long for ordinary purposes tuck't into his coat; an arquebus on his shoulder, and on his thigh a scymitar; on one side of the saddle a petronnelle, on the other a straight sword and, hanging by it, either a little axe or a Hungarian mace, or both. On his back bows and arrows."

Truly a portentous outfit!

The *piadés* need no particular description as they were recruited and served under practically the same conditions as the *spahis*, the difference being that they were foot soldiers.

Of the artillery also there is not very much to say. Originally the Turks borrowed this arm from their Christian enemies, and for centuries the arsenals on the Bosphorus were under the charge of renegades. They developed it rapidly, however, as they did all instruments of war, and soon outpaced the original inventors, so that by the fifteenth century they were better equipped with heavy artillery than any of their rivals. The size of some of the guns was enormous. At the siege of Constantinople when guns were sent to the Bosphorus from Adrianople—then the capital of the Turks in Europe—teams of 150 yoke of oxen were used to haul single pieces. The batteries placed to guard the Narrows at the Dardanelles were notorious. An English diplomat who visited them on his way to Constantinople in 1827 declares that one of the cannon was of 2-foot calibre and threw a solid stone projectile weighing a quarter of a ton. No unworthy ancestor, forsooth, of the monstrous " Asiatic Annie" of evil memory.

A considerable part of the Turkish army was made up of irregular troops. The chief of these were the *azabs* and *akinjis*, who, as cavalry and infantry respectively, played the *rôle* of "shock troops" and were mercilessly sacrificed in action in order to prepare the ground for a charge by the invincible janissaries. Another and very extraordinary corps were the volunteers known as *delis* (*anglicé*, "Mad-caps"), who, under the influence of religious fanaticism, used to offer themselves for any particularly desperate enterprise, and of whom it was said that not a single one had ever shown his back to the enemy, whatever the odds. The dress worn by these " Mad-caps" was of an outrageous design, intended, like the masks of the old Chinese warriors, to strike fear into the heart of the enemy. It consisted of a dolman and breeches made of a lion or bear skin with the hair turned outwards, and a bonnet of leopard's skin with a pair of eagle's wings sewn on in such a way as to stand upright on either side. Another pair of wings projected from their shields, so that the whole effect was that of a moving mass of fur and feathers—even their horses being covered with the skins of various wild animals. Their usual weapons were a scimitar, a club and a long pike.

A "MADCAP"

From Nicolay's *Pérégrinations faictes en la Turquie*, 1577

The Tartar auxiliaries—the last of the five elements composing the Turkish armies—came from the Crimea and the northern shores of the Black Sea. The Tartars were hereditary allies of the Turks to whom they are related by religion, race and language. The Tartar *Khans*, heirs-presumptive to the throne of Turkey in the event of the Ottoman dynasty becoming extinguished, were therefore bound to assist the Sultans with troops in all their campaigns against Christian nations. The bond was made doubly secure by the retention of the reigning *Khan's* eldest son at the Sultan's court, where he lived as a permanent hostage for his father's loyalty. Hordes of Tartar cavalry accompanied the Turkish armies when they marched into Europe, and acted as scouts and skirmishers on the flanks. They were wild, undisciplined horsemen who spent their whole lives in the saddle and whose food was mare's milk, caviare and meat "cooked" by being placed in slabs under their horses' girths till it was bruised to a suitable state of tenderness. In enemy country they advanced in loose order ahead, and on the wings of, the regular army where they ambushed bodies of the enemy and pillaged and murdered with complete impartiality the inhabitants of. the country and any unfortunate stragglers from the ranks of their own allies. Their services were paid by a free licence to loot and to them fell the lion's share of the plunder. In a later page of the present volume we have a picture of them in action as given by an English gentleman who fought against them in the Polish wars.

CHAPTER IV

A PALACE AUDIENCE

At daybreak on Aug. 15, 1682, there was a great stir at the old Venetian *bailaggio* in Pera. H.E. Giorgio Battista Donado, Senator of Venice and Ambassador Plenipotentiary of the Most Serene Republic, was preparing for his first audience with the Sultan Mohammed IV which was to open the way to the resumption of amity between Turkey and Venice after the long interruption of the Candian war.

The ambassador and his suite had, in point of fact, arrived at Constantinople more than a year before, but matters had been delayed by a hitch of a very typical character. For years past it had been the custom of the Grand Vizir, the notorious Black Mustafa, to levy a heavy tax upon each new ambassador on the occasion of his first presentation to the Sultan, and as all petitions for an audience passed through his hands the petitioners had no choice but to submit to the robbery. The proud senator, however, met these rapacious demands on his purse with an absolute refusal which enraged the Vizir and consequently barred his access to the palace. Fortunately the Sultan's favourite son-in-law, who suffered from a long-standing malady, had been cured by the embassy doctor and showed his gratitude by befriending his master. A short cut to the emperor's ear was thus found. Mohammed, yielding to the persuasion of his favourite, agreed to receive the ambassador and the arrangements for the audience were complete.

Now that the day had arrived, everything was ordered in the finest style and with that degree of pomp and circumstance which the stately traditions of Venice demanded. As soon as it was light the subordinate staff gathered in the large courtyard of the embassy where the major-domo was already parading the escort. The latter consisted of an Albanian bodyguard, a score of Croatian couriers resplendent in crimson liveries, twelve chamberlains in dresses of orange satin cut in the Turkish fashion and an equal number of grooms in pearl-coloured silk leading the horses; the usual guard of janissaries attached to a foreign ambassador to the Porte completed the party.

Soon the ambassador himself appeared followed by his "household," that is to say his secretaries, chaplains, physician, surgeon, man-of-law and dragomans. These last included several young men from the special school at Venice where youths were taught the Turkish language and trained for the duties of diplomatic dragoman in Turkey. The name of one of these was Antonio Benetti and it is to his memoirs[1] that we are indebted for this account of the proceedings.

When all was ready the little party, augmented now by a contingent of the better class merchants belonging to the Venetian colony, left the *bailaggio* and riding down the steep cobbled street which leads through Galata—the ancient Genoese quarter—reached the edge of the Golden Horn. There was no "Galata Bridge" in those days, but a fleet of *caïques* was drawn up at the water's edge waiting to ferry them across to Stambul. These delicate craft, built like a flat-hulled gondola with a cushioned space amidships for the passen-

---

[1] *Viaggi a Constantinopoli*, published at Venice in 1688.

gers, are the typical pleasure-boat of the Bosphorus and the most graceful things afloat. A special boat with fourteen rowers, gilded woodwork and velvet hangings, its cushions covered with gold-lace antimacassars, carried the ambassador across followed by his party in smaller *caïques* and their horses in clumsier built *maünas*.

The *Chaoush Bashi*—the Grand Master of Ceremonies—was waiting to receive them on the further shore, and after the usual salutations a procession was formed to march to the palace. Fifty picked mounts from the royal stables had been sent, with the Master of the Horse, for the use of the ambassador and his staff, and their own beasts which they had brought with them were led riderless, in obedience to a curious Turkish custom, at the head of the procession. It was a glittering cavalcade that wound its way first through the wharves and ship-building yards, then through the covered bazars and up the narrow streets which mount the first of Stambul's seven hills. The splendid figure of the Venetian senator in his dress of crimson taffetas faced with gold brocade and lined with ermine riding alone behind the *Chaoush Bashi* with a *bostanji* walking on either side and followed by his staff clad in the fashion of their day in tight *juste-au-corps* brought even the impassive Turkish populace flocking to the route, and the close-packed shingle houses with their projecting bays of lattice-work were crowded with onlookers curious to see the envoy of their great maritime rival.

Having reached the open space in front of Santa Sofia the procession turned in at the main gate of the seraglio, passing through a large archway under a gate-tower which broke the massive line of the walls and gave entrance into the first court of the royal palace.

This court, which was of huge dimensions, served as a parade-ground for the household troops and as it marked the limit beyond which no horses were allowed to pass, the *cortège* dismounted and leaving their horses with those of the Vizirs who had already arrived continued towards the second court on foot.

Sitting on a bench within the gate-way separating the two courts was the Agha of the janissaries with twenty-eight of his colonels in their pointed brocade hats with three large white plumes and three smaller black ones set fan-wise in front, together with the commander of the *spahis* with a group of his principal officers in brilliant uniforms of green satin and cloth-of-gold.

After exchanging salutes with both these military "big-wigs," Donado and his following passed on into the inner court. Here they found themselves in a wide expanse surrounded on all sides by cloisters and containing a grassy park dotted about with clumps of trees under which tame stags and other beasts were grazing. The place was filled with some 8000 janissaries passing the time in idle amusements.

As they walked along a path leading across the park they were startled to hear a number of the janissaries suddenly raise a terrific shout and dash tumultuously towards a corner of the court thundering like a charge of cavalry, with their heavy iron-shod shoes rattling on the stone paving of the cloisters. At first they feared that an outburst of fanaticism had been let loose against them, but were soon reassured when they saw that the object of this furious onslaught was nothing but a row of tin cans which had just been brought into the court and set down on the stones of the cloisters. The cans were full of rice and chicken broth and contained the janissaries' dinner. The scene which ensued is best described in Benetti's own language which I will render as nearly as I can into English: "Then these barbarians began to gobble their food, silencing their tongues meanwhile but making a deafening clatter as they beat the tins with their hands, and all the time they ate so ravenously that they beslobbered their faces all over, and in less time than it takes to light a candle every drop of the soup had vanished."

On the side of the court furthest from the gateway by which our friends had entered stood the *divan* chamber. The *divan* was an early Turkish institution nearly resembling our cabinet meetings, being a conference of the principal Ministers of State to discuss all important matters of government. Originally an informal council of the Sultan and his chief officers, it had become stereotyped as time went on, and at the period of which we are speaking was a regular assembly, meeting two or three times a week, of certain of the highest officials including the two *Cadileskers* (the Chief Justices respectively of Europe and Asia), the Treasurer-General and the Vizirs responsible for finance, justice and foreign affairs. The president of the *divan* was the Grand Vizir. In earlier days it had been the Sultan; but the story goes that an Anatolian rustic entering one day to ask for justice in some trivial affair and wishing to make his plea in the highest quarter, shouted in his rough peasant way *kiminez padishah dir*, "which of you there is the Sultan?"; whereafter in order to avoid further. offences of the sort against his royal dignity the Sultan ceased to attend the *divan* and deputed the Grand Vizir in his stead.

A *CADILESKER*
From Nicolay's *Pérégrinations faictes en la Turquie,* 1577

Turkish procedure required that before the personal audience the ambassador should be presented to the *divan*, so His Excellency, leaving his followers in the court, advanced alone to the chamber, bowing profoundly to the door of the royal apartments which he passed on the way as sailors salute the quarterdeck on a man-o'-war. Entering, he greeted the Grand Vizir —whom his chief dragoman, sent on ahead for the purpose, had already placated to some degree with handsome presents—and was offered, in deference to European habits, a chair to sit on.

The *divan* chamber was a large square room roofed with a dome painted with flowers in the gaudy rococo style much admired by the Turk, which terribly ruins the interior harmony of some of the finest mosques in Stambul. Three large windows gave light to the room and a couple of feet above the head of the Grand Vizir as he sat cross-legged on the daïs was a little gilt grille with silk curtains, behind which the Sultan sat when he wished to hear, or take part in, the proceedings of the council. Copies of the Koran, the Bible and the Talmud lay ready to hand for use in "swearing in" witnesses when called to give evidence at a meeting. All the members of the *divan* were present, ten in all, including the *Cadileskers*, while the *Defterdar* or Minister of Finance, the *Chaoush Bashi* and the head of the *Capujis* or Door-keepers were also in attendance.

A curious little ceremony was being enacted at the moment that the ambassador arrived. The Grand Vizir had just affixed his seal to an order on the Treasury for a large sum for the payment of the troops which he handed to the chief *Capuji* to take to the Sultan for his ratification. The *Capuji*, kissing his hand, took the paper and carried it out of the room, holding it at the height of his shoulder. He soon returned from the royal apartments now holding the paper, sanctified by the imperial *tughra*, on a level with his head, all the Vizirs rising from their seats and bowing profoundly as he passed. The Grand Vizir received back the order with every mark of reverence, kissing the document and laying it on his bowed head before proceeding to open the seal and read it out to the company. As soon as he had done so, *chaoushes* appeared carrying 800 purses of gold which were counted and checked in the presence of all by the Paymaster-General. The janissary *chorbajis* then entered to draw the pay for their various "chambers." They first went up to the Grand Vizir and kissed the hem of his cloak—a performance made somewhat difficult by the enormous plumes in their hats, to avoid thrusting which into the Grand Vizir's face they had to contort themselves to most unnatural angles. Afterwards they stood in a row while the *Defterdar* handed to each the appointed number of purses, on receiving which the officer retired outside and called the men of his chamber to carry them to their quarters, whereupon—to the great entertainment of Benetti and his companions—a scramble ensued, even wilder than the rush for the soup-cans, those in front slipping on the flagstones and tripping those behind so that in a minute the ground was covered with struggling janissaries and littered with their shoes and plumed hats.

To return to the proceedings within the *divan*, the distribution of pay being over, the next item on the agenda was taken, consisting of the bestowal of a fur-lined dress of honour (the Turkish equivalent of an "O.B.E.") on the *Defterdar* and the Head of the

Customs. With the decoration of these two officials, the formal business of the *divan*, of which the ambassador had to remain a passive spectator, was finished and preparations were made for a banquet in his honour. Some cloths were laid on the floor and the ambassador's personal suite having been invited inside, they sat down to eat, the ambassador himself sharing a "table" on a raised daïs with the Grand Vizir, his secretaries dining with the *Cadileskers*, the chaplains with the *Defterdar* and so on. On each "table" was placed a silver salver of huge dimensions raised on a short pedestal, and on this the *sofrajis* laid the dishes one by one, surrounding them with a circle of little platters full of all sorts of spices and condiments. The dishes themselves were made of a kind of rough porcelain with a slightly greenish hue reputed among the Turks to have the property of neutralizing any poison which might have insinuated itself into the viands. Each guest was provided with a napkin and a single spoon with a very long handle, their Turkish *vis-à-vis* dispensing of course with such superfluities. The number and variety of the courses is well-nigh incredible. One hundred and thirty dishes of fish, game, meat, risottos, savouries, sweets and ices succeeded each other in an endless procession, while varieties of sweet sherbets supplied the necessary liquid accompaniment.

When this colossal repast was at length over and the diners' hands had been sprinkled with rose-water, the guests were led to a loggia outside the *divan*. Here a ceremony took place which formed the invariable prelude to an audience with the Sultan. Officials arrived with a number of handsome *kaftans*, or fur-lined cloaks, and threw them over the shoulders of the ambassador and those members of his suite who were to accompany him into the presence. Although this feasting and costly arraying of the guests were the outward and visible signs—or perhaps one should say, the conventional symbols—of the spirit of true hospitality which was firmly implanted in the Turks as in all other races of nomadic origins, the effect must have been a good deal discounted by the guests' knowledge of the real feelings of their hosts. Benetti, not unnaturally perhaps, lays but little stress on the undignified position of a Christian representative at the Porte and the boundless arrogance which he met with at court, but we can judge how it was by the following account, from another source, of the formula regularly used between the Grand Signior and his chief Vizir whenever a Christian ambassador came to the palace for an audience. The Vizir would first announce the arrival of the envoy, whereupon the Sultan would reply, "feed and clothe the dog and bring him in to me." Sometime later, when the ambassador and his followers had been feasted and enveloped in *kaftans* in the way described above, the Vizir would return and say, "the infidel is fed and clothed and he now craves leave to lick the dusk beneath Your Majesty's throne," "then," answered the Sultan, "let the hound enter."

The Venetian envoys, who were unaware, we will hope for the sake of their self-respect, of the insulting dialogue which had passed in relation to themselves, were now formed up into line and, preceded by the Grand Vizir, the *Cadileskers* and the other pashas of the *divan*, were ushered towards the audience chamber. Just as they passed the Guard of White Eunuchs, which stood at the door, they were fallen upon by a number of *capujis*, two of whom gripped each of them under either arm and pushed, rather than led, them into the Sultan's presence.

This seemingly erratic proceeding needs another short digression to explain it. On the day that the Turks defeated the Serbs on the field of Kossovo, Sultan Murad I was sitting in his tent just after the battle had ended when Milosh, a Serbian patriot, who saw that all hopes for his country had vanished, came to the tent and asked leave to address a petition to the Sultan. The Ottoman sultans in those early days were not hemmed around as they afterwards were, and the suppliant was allowed to enter. In an instant he drew a dagger which he had concealed on his person and stabbed the Sultan to death. Hence, by Turkish tradition, arose the custom of never allowing a stranger to enter the presence of the Sultan unless held by trusted attendants. Sceptical historians have, it is true, tried to discredit tradition and have traced the custom to a similar procedure current at the Byzantine courts; for myself, I prefer the Turkish derivation.

Thus propelled like automata, and buried in their furs, the representatives of Venice entered the room where the Sultan awaited them. Round the room hung Persian carpets and in a corner stood the famous throne with its panels of beaten gold and magnificent pearl inlay. The throne was shadowed by a splendid canopy incrusted with rubies and sapphires and supporting a mesh of strings of pearls which hung round the Sultan's head, the portion immediately over him containing the largest pearls and ending in a fringe of emeralds. An overlay of fine-drawn gold wire set with glowing carbuncles adorned the arms of the throne.

Sitting in the midst of this splendour was the Grand Signior himself, his dress a blaze of precious stones of every description, while he wore on his head the imperial headdress consisting of a small turban with a magnificent three-branched diamond tiara and an aigret feather in the centre.

The Grand Vizir had taken up his post behind the Sultan where he stood with his eyes lowered as though unable to endure the dazzling radiance of the monarch, when the ambassador's attendants brought him to a halt three paces short of the throne. There, in accordance with the fixed procedure, he handed his credentials to a pasha standing by, who passed them to the Grand Vizir who, in his turn, laid them on the Sultan's knee. This done, he delivered a short set speech expressing the desire of the Most Serene Republic to live thenceforward on terms of amity with the Ottoman Emperor and the hope that all causes of offence between the two Powers, in particular the inroads of the corsairs on Venetian shipping, having now been suppressed, both nations might reap the inestimable benefits of peace.

The Sultan's reply to this eloquent oration consisted of two short words "*Euïle olsun,*" "be it so!" and without further ado the ambassador was forcibly backed to the door and hustled out with his suite behind him. A military band of fifes and drums escorted them back to the embassy, followed soon afterwards by an army of servants carrying return gifts from the Sultan[1].

[1] Benetti does not record the nature of the Venetian ambassador's gifts to the Sultan; but it may not be out of place to quote the list of presents which Mr William Harebone, the first English ambassador to the Porte, took from Elizabeth to Murad III. They are as follows: "twelve fine broad clothes, two pieces of fine holland, tenne pieces of plate double gilt,

Thus were diplomatic relations restored between Venice and Turkey.

one case of candlesticks, the case thereof was very large, and three foot high and more, two very great cannes or pots, and one lesser, one basin and ewer, two poppinjayes of silver, the one with two heads; they were to drinke in : two bottles with chaines, three faire mastifs in coats of redde cloth, three spaniels, two bloodhounds, one common hunting hound, two greyhounds, two little dogges in coats of silke : one clocke valued at five hundred pounds sterling : over it was a forest with trees of silver, among the which were deere chased with dogs, and men on horsebacke following, men drawing of water, others carrying mine oare on barrowes : on the toppe of the clocke stood a castle, and on the castle a mill. All these were of silver. And the clocke was round beset with jewels."

CHAPTER V

AN EMBASSY TO THE GRAND TURKE

(1)

In the year 1553 Sultan Suleyman the Magnificent
was at truce with the Holy Roman Empire for almost
the first time in more than a quarter of a century. He
had inaugurated the most brilliant reign in Turkish
history some thirty years before by crushing the forces
of Hungary in the bloody battle of Mohacz, when
King Louis with his entire company of bishops and
knights had met their death in a vain, though heroic,
charge against his invincible janissaries. Following up
his victory he had pressed on through Hungary into
the heart of Austria and laid siege to Vienna. For a
moment the fate of Christendom had seemed to tremble
in the balance ; but the tide turned and, failing to take
the city, Suleyman had retired again to his own territories after arranging a compromise with the Archduke
Ferdinand, heir of King Louis, which left his own
nominee, John Zapolya, on the Hungarian throne.
Zapolya had died and an effort by the German armies
to recover the lost dominions having ended in disaster,
the truce had been signed between the Sultan, Charles
the Fifth and the Archduke, Ferdinand binding himself for the time being to recognise the Turkish claim
over the greater part of Hungary and to pay a humili-
ating tribute.

It was at this juncture of events that Malvezius, Ferdinand's ambassador, received from Suleyman proposals for a definite peace, and returned to Vienna with the terms in his pocket. He had just started back with Ferdinand's answer when he found himself suddenly laid low by a fatal disease contracted originally during a two-years' incarceration in the Seven Towers to which he had been consigned some time before as the result of a fatuous attempt to hoodwink the Grand Signior. It is at this point that Busbequius, the hero of the following pages, enters upon the scene.

Busbequius, whose Christian name was Andreas, was born in Flanders in 1522, being the bastard son of a nobleman who secured his legitimization by a special rescript of Charles V. His education was as liberal and cosmopolitan as could be desired for the training of an accomplished diplomat ; he had mastered a dozen languages at an early age and matriculated in turn at the Universities of Paris, Louvain, Venice, Padua and Bologna. When he was twenty-one years of age he was attached by Ferdinand to a special embassy sent to London to represent him at the marriage of Queen Mary with Philip of Spain. Returning from this mission he was surprised at Lille by an urgent despatch from Vienna appointing him to replace Malvezius as Imperial Ambassador of Constantinople. He left Lille on November 13, 1553, posted with all speed across the Continent, received his orders from the Emperor, snatched a bare two-days' interview with his dying predecessor, and hurrying on reached Gran, the Turkish frontier garrison on the Danube, in the first days of December, where he was met by a Turkish escort. At this point we will let Busbequius himself

take up the narrative, quoting from the English translation (published in 1694) of his *Epistolae* :

" As soon as the Turks saw me to draw near," he
says, "they rode up to me, and saluted me by my coach
side : thus we passed on a while together, discoursing
interchangeably one with another, (for I had a little
Youth for my Interpreter.) I expected no other Convoy,
but when we descended into a low Valley, I saw myself on a sudden, surrounded with a Party of about
a hundred and fifty Horse. It was a very pleasant
Spectacle to a Man, unaccustomed to see such Sights,
for their Bucklers and Spears were curiously Painted,
their Sword-handles bedeck'd with Jewels, their Plumes
of Feathers party-coloured, and the Coverings of their
Heads were twisted with round Windings as white as
Snow ; their Apparel was Purple-coloured, or at least
a dark Blue ; They rode on stately Praunsers, adorn'd
with most beautiful Trappings. Their Commanders
came up to me, and after friendly Salutation they bid
me Welcome, and asked me, How I had fared on my
Journey ? I answered them as I thought fit ; and thus
they led me to Gran."

Busbequius's first experiences on Turkish soil were
not very propitious. He soon found, somewhat to his
disgust, that the Turkish conception of honouring a
travelling guest was to provide the choicest stabling
and fodder for the horses together with the most
meagre board and lodging for their master, who was
expected to content himself, according to local custom,
with planks for his bed and an invariable diet of *pillau* for
his stomach. The ambassadorial party were accom-
modated at the free hostels scattered along the road
which had been built and endowed by the Mother or

sisters of the Sultan and his predecessors—the only persons privileged to indulge their charity in this shape —where a common hospitality was dispensed to all wayfarers alike, whether Moslem, Christian, Jew; Pasha, merchant or mendicant. Another cause of much grumbling among Busbequius's retinue was the absence of wine in a Moslem country. The Ambassador himself had taken care to provide an ample supply of good liquor for his own use, but as he kept a jealous eye on the flagons which filled the spare corners of his coach, his followers had to scour the villages far and wide in search of Christian wine vendors. Busbequius seems in this respect to have shown more liberality to strangers than to his own folk, for he describes a dinner party given to the local Turks at his first stopping place at which his guests found his wines so much to their liking that when he parted from them at midnight they lay round the table dead drunk to a man. Philosophising on the subject of the Moslem attitude towards alcohol, he illustrates his point by one of the quaint little anecdotes which dot the pages of his letters and lend to them so much of their special charm. "At Constantinople" he writes "I saw an Old Man, who, after he had taken a Cup of Wine in his Hand to Drink, us'd first to make a hideous Noise; I asked his Friends, Why he did so? They answered me, that, by this Outcry, he did, as it were, warn his Soul to retire to some secret Corner of his Body, or else, wholly to Emigrate, and pass out of it, that she might not be guilty of that Sin which he was about to commit, nor be defiled with the Wine that he was about to guzzle down."

An untoward incident occurred again on the arrival

of the mission at Buda. The Turkish Governor of the town happening to be indisposed at the time sent to Busbequius and begged him to lend the services of his private physician, a gentleman bearing the somewhat inauspicious name of Dr Quackquelben ; whether it was that the Turkish constitution baffled the good doctor's powers of diagnosis or through a stroke of sheer bad luck, the Pasha after swallowing the prescribed dose incontinently grew worse and on the following day came near to expiring ; it was only after the greatest efforts that the unfortunate physician pulled the patient round and so saved himself and his master from a grave suspicion of murder.

Leaving Buda, Busbequius shipped his horses, coaches and all his "family" (as he calls his suite) on rafts on the Danube and proceeded downstream to Belgrade, as being not only the quickest route but also the most secure from attack by brigands. He presently found, however, that the risks of navigation on the Danube were at least as great as those of robbery on the roads, for the temerity of the Turks was such—he writes—that they would sally forth in the mistiest weather, the darkest night or the highest gale. The fairway was often blocked by water-mills or stumps of old trees and he was once awakened at midnight by the sound of splitting timbers to find that his raft (which was being towed by a 24-oared pinnace) had hurtled against some such obstacle. He implored the boatmen to have more regard for the safety of their passengers, but had to content himself with the laconic reply that their lives were in the hands of Allah and "he might go back to bed if he would."

The journey through the Serbian vilayets occupies

only a few pages of the ambassador's letters. His attention was chiefly attracted by the forests of poles which he saw planted in the churchyards as he passed, bearing pictures of stags, hinds and other fleet-footed animals. The explanation he received from the natives was that when a Serbian woman died, her husband or, if unmarried, her father, often erected a monument in this form to commemorate the alacrity and diligence which his wife or daughter had shewn in the execution of her household duties. In the passage through Bulgaria it was the costume of the peasant women that particularly caught his eye, which is not to be wondered at when we read the following description of their dress —though it is less easy to understand why the sight of these strangely apparelled females should have reminded him, as he affirms, of "Clytemnestra in the flourishing days of Troy."

"I must not omit," says he, "to acquaint you with the Habit of these Bulgarian Women. They commonly wear nothing but a Smock or Shift, made of no finer Linnèn-Thread, than that we make Sacks of. And yet, these coarse Garments are wrought by them, with several sorts of strip'd Needle-work, after a homely Fashion.

"But that which I most of all admired in them, was the Tower, which they wore on their Heads, for such was the Form of their Hats. They were made of Straw, braided with webs over them. In the space interjacent between their upper and lower Part, they hang Pieces of Coin, little Pictures or Images, small parcels of painted Glass, or whatever is resplendent, though never so mean, which are accounted very ornamental among them.

" Those kind of Hats makes them look taller, and also more matron-like, though they are easily blown off their Heads, by a Blast of Wind, or by any light Motion they fall off themselves."

Early in the New Year Busbequius arrived at Constantinople, only to find that Suleyman had been called away from the capital by domestic disturbances and was in quarters four hundred miles away at Amadia, a town in Armenia lying between Sivas and the Black Sea port of Samsūn. Letters were at once despatched to the Sultan announcing the arrival of Ferdinand's ambassador and asking for instructions as to his movements. In the meantime Busbequius settled down to see the sights of the city and its surroundings. To the beauty of the landscapes amid which the city stands Busbequius appears to have been as blind as most of the writers of his time. He spares hardly a word for those incomparable harmonies of line and colour which have rejoiced the heart of those of us who, like the old Fleming, have been familiar with Stamboul's mosques and *serais* and old grey walls and have looked across from the wooded heights of Asia to its perfect contours of dome, minaret, battlement and tower blending with the dark hillsides and the silvery gleam of the Bosphorus flowing below.

The obsession for classical antiquities which marked the age in which Busbequius lived had but a moderate hold on him. His letters contain brief sketches of the principal monuments dating from Byzantine days: Santa Sophia, the Hippodrome, the serpent pillar and the obelisk of Thothmes and he mentions *en passant* the collection which he made of Greek coins, describing especially his horrified indignation on finding that a brazier of Stamboul had, just before his arrival, melted down an entire roomful of antique coins and medals to make pots and pans. On the other hand, he took the keenest interest in all his *living* surroundings and never tires of describing the customs of his Christian and Moslem neighbours. A strong bent for natural history had led to his bringing with him an artist whose sole business it was to paint all the uncommon beasts and flowers met with on their travels. His own letters, however, contain as attractive sketches as any painter could give of the animals they met with on their travels, as an example of which let me quote a passage in which he describes a visit to the Sultan's private Zoo:

"At Constantinople I saw several Sorts of Wild Beasts, such as Lynxes, Cat-a-Mountains, Panthers, Leopards and Lyons; but they were so gentle and tame that I saw one of the Keepers pull a Sheep out of a Lyon's mouth, so that he only moistened his Jaws with the Blood without devouring it. I also saw a young Elephant so wanton that she would dance and play at Ball. Sure you cannot chuse but laugh when I tell you of an Elephant's dancing and playing at Ball; but why may you not believe me as well as Seneca, who tells us of one that could dance upon a rope? Or of Pliny, who speaks of another that understood Greek? But that you may not think me an egregious Forger, give me leave to explain myself: When this elephant was bid to dance, she did so caper and quiver with her whole body, and interchangeably move her feet, that she seemed to represent a kind of jig; and as for playing at Ball, she very prettily took up the Ball in her Trunk and sent it packing hither and thither as we do with the Palm of the Hand."

The "Camelopardus" was, one gathers from contemporary writings, a beast which excited a great deal of discussion among naturalists of the sixteenth century. Tales of travellers who had come across the giraffe in Africa were received with a good deal of scepticism on account of the unparelleled proportions attributed to the animal, and many of the scientific writers of the day affected to treat it as a fabulous monster. It must therefore have been a great disappointment to Busbequius that he just missed a chance of seeing one of these creatures in the flesh. She had lately been an inmate of the Zoo but had died shortly before his arrival at Constantinople; in his ardent pursuit of science, however, Busbequius persuaded the Turks to disinter her and made an exhaustive anatomical examination of the animal's remains.

He indulges also in the favourite "scientific" speculations of the old travellers to Constantinople: the causes of the double current of the Bosphorus, why the waters of the Black Sea are salt and whether the floating islands mentioned by certain classical authors really exist. It is, by the way, interesting to note the apologetic tone adopted by Busbequius in common with his contemporaries whenever venturing an opinion at variance with that of Pliny and other classical authorities; it was indeed an uncritical age which hesitated to assume in itself any knowledge in advance of that possessed by the world of 1500 years before!

The messengers sent to Suleyman to announce Busbequius's arrival returned in due course with orders that he was to proceed to Amadia. He, his horses, coaches and baggage train are "wafted' across the Bosphorus and the long land journey across half the length of Asia Minor begins. Now again it is the variety of wild animals seen on the way which chiefly attracts the traveller's notice. First the vast number of tortoises which strew the ground on the Asiatic coast "stalking" he writes, "over all the Field without any Fear at all." "We had certainly seized upon many of them as a prey grateful to our Palates had it not been for the Turkish Guides whom we were afraid to disoblige; for if they had seen any of them brought to our Table, much more if they had touched them, they would have thought themselves so defiled that I know not how many Washings would not have been needed to cleanse their imagined Pollution." To which he somewhat callously adds: "I kept one Tortoise by me a great while which had two Heads and would have lived much longer had I been as careful of it as I might."

Concerning the hyenas, which abounded in those parts of Asia Minor, he has the following surprising yarn to tell: "The Turks have a Tradition that the Hyena, which they call the Zirtlan, understands what Men say to one another. The Antients affirm'd that they could also imitate Man's Voice, and thereupon Hunters catch them by this Wile. They find out her Den, which they may easily do by the heap of Bones lying by it; and then one of them goes in with a Rope, leaving the other end of the Rope in the Hands of his Fellows without; and when he is creeping in he cries with a loud Voice, *Joctur, Joctur, Ucala*[1] i.e. 'She is not here, She is not here!' or 'I cannot find her!' whereupon the Hyena, thinking she is not discovered, lies

---

[1] Busbequius's scraps of Turkish are not always very intelligible. They have probably got a good deal mutilated in the process of transliteration and subsequent transcription by the English translator.

close, and he ties the end of the rope round her leg;
and then he goes forth, still crying, 'I cannot find her!'
but when he is escaped quite out of the Hole, he cries
out loudly 'she is within, she is within!' which the
Hyena hearing and understanding the meaning of it,
leaps out thinking to escape; but when they hold her
back by the Rope tied to her leg, and either kill her, or
if they use care and Diligence, take her alive, for she
is a fierce Creature and defends herself desperately."

Thirty days after leaving Constantinople the ambassador's party reached Amadia, then the chief city of
Cappadocia, a strong place overhung by a high hill on
the top of which was a castle garrisoned by a Turkish
force maintained there to repulse raids by the Persians
who occasionally penetrated even to this distance within
their neighbour's territory. Busbequius and his suite
were first introduced to the Grand Vizir and chief Pashas
and an audience with the Sultan was duly arranged.
When the day came Busbequius was introduced into
Suleyman's presence supported under each arm by a
Court Chamberlain in accordance with the ancient custom the origin of which has already been explained in
an earlier chapter of this book. Having thus laboriously
arrived at the goal of his journeyings, the ambassador
prepared to deliver himself of the message entrusted
to him by the Archduke Ferdinand. The scene is
described as follows:

"The Sultan sate on a low Throne, not above a
foot from the ground, but all covered over with rich
Tapistries and with Cushions exquisitely wrought. His
Bow and Arrows lay by his Side while he himself looked
sternly upon us; and yet there was a certain Majesty
mixed with the Severity in his Countenance. After we

had kissed his Hand, we were led backward to the opposite part of the Room, for the Turks count it an unmannerly Thing to turn any of their Back-parts upon their Prince. From thence I had liberty to declare my Master's commands. But they suited not Soliman's lofty and imperious Spirit, who thought that nothing ought to be denied him; so that he, as disdaining them, said nothing but *Giusel, Giusel*; that is, Well, Well. And so we were dismissed to our Lodgings."

While things went thus badly for Ferdinand's embassy, a mission from the Shah of Persia which had reached Amadia at about the same time, bound on a similar errand, met with a far different reception. Suleyman needed a respite from the Persian wars and readily accepted the peace proposals brought by the Shah's emissary with a mass of princely presents, which included "many choice sorts of Hangings, Babylonian Tents, gallant Horse-trappings and Saddles, Scymiters made at Damascus, whose Handles were studded with Jewels, and Shields of beautiful Workmanship, together with that which exceeded all, namely the Alcoran which is a counted the most noble Present of all."

The Persian negotiations having been speedily concluded, the ambassador was offered a sumptuous banquet by Ali Pasha, the Deputy Grand Vizir, in a garden outside the town. "The Table," relates Busbequius, "at which the Bashaw and the Persian Ambassador sate was covered over with a Canopy and the Dishes were served up after this manner. There were one hundred Youths which attended, like Waiters, all of them alike habited. First of all they entered one by one at a small distance from each other, till the Train of them reached up to the Table where the Guests were sitting. They had nothing at all in their Hands, that so they might not be hindered in saluting the Guests which was done in this manner; they laid their Hands on their Thighs and bowed their Heads downwards to the Ground. When this ceremony was performed, then he that stood next the Kitchen took a Dish and gave it to the next Page immediately before him, and he handed it to a Third and he to a Fourth and so from one to another until it came to him that stood next the Table, who delivered it to the Hands of the Gentleman-Server, who placed it on the Table. And thus one hundred Dishes or more were served up in excellent order without any Noise at all. And when this was done, then these Waiters or Pages saluted the Guests a second time and so retired in the same order they came in."

It is greatly to Busbequius's credit that the invidious distinction shewn in the treatment accorded to himself and to the Persian evokes no echo of resentment in his letters : but the motive behind the Sultan's behaviour lay, as he was aware, not in any personal animosity against himself but in Suleyman's wish to give visible evidence of his determination not to treat with Ferdinand on any other terms than those of a lord dealing with a suppliant. The German terms of peace were such as might be offered by a monarch to his peer and had small chance of acceptance by the Sultan in his present frame of mind. The most that Busbequius was able to secure was a six-months' truce (for fighting had broken out again since he left Vienna), and having accomplished this, he decided to return to his master to acquaint him by word of mouth with Suleyman's terms for a permanent treaty. " I was then," he writes, "again introduced into Solyman's presence and had two large embroidered

Vests, reaching down to my Ancles, clap'd onto me; they were so heavy that I could hardly stand under them. My Family also, that attended me, were all clad with silken Garments of divers Colours. In this Posture I stalked along, like Agamemnon or some such piece of Gravity in a Tragedy, and so I took leave of the Emperor, having first received Letters from him to my Master, seal'd and wrap'd up in Cloth of Gold. And thus, after we had taken our leaves of the Bashaws, I and my Colleagues departed from Amadia."

Before closing this chapter of his narrative, Busbequius gives us a sketch of Suleyman the Magnificent. "If you ask me," says he, "what manner of man Solyman is, I'll tell you. He is an ancient Man, his countenance and the mien of his Body very majestic, well becoming the Dignity which he wears; he is frugal and temperate though he might have taken a greater Liberty to himself by the Rules of his own Religion, so that his very enemies can object nothing against him on that Account, but that he was too uxurious and that his over-indulgence to his Wife made him give way to the Death of his Son Mustapha [whom he caused to be bow-strung for an alleged attempt to incite rebellion]. Yet even that Crime was vulgarly imputed to the Ascendant that Roxolana had over him by reason of her Inchantments and Love-Potions.

"He is now sixty Years of Age, and for a Man of his Years he enjoys a moderate proportion of Health; and yet his Countenance doth discover that he carries about him some hidden Disease, 'tis thought a Gangrene or Ulcer in the Thigh; but at solemn Audiences of Ambassadors he hath a Fucus to paint his Cheeks with, that he may appear sound and healthy to them and thereupon be more dreaded by foreign Princes, their Masters. Methought I discovered some such thing at my Dismission, for his Countenance was as sour when I left him as at my first Audience."

The two ambassadors left Amadia on the same day, parting outside the walls to go East and West each to his native land. Within a fortnight the cumbrous train of coaches rumbled once more under the massive gateway in those city walls which just a century before had crumbled before the battering of Mohammed's guns and let in his sanguinary hosts over the trampled corpse of the last of the Greek Emperors.

As they left the town behind them the party came upon a sight which must have made the proud but kind-hearted ambassador grind his teeth with impotent rage. Waggon after waggon-load of girls and boys came pouring along the road, all of them Christian captives on their way from Hungary to Constantinople to be sold in the slave-markets. "There was no Distinction of Age; Old and Young were driven in Herds or Companies, or else were tied in a long Chain, as we use to tail Horses when we carry them to Fairs. When I beheld this woful Sight, I could not forbear weeping and bemoaning the unhappy State of poor Christendom."

After no worse experiences than a surfeit of carp consumed on a fast-day at Belgrade and a narrow escape from brigands when crossing a ford, the company arrived at Buda. Here the same ill-fortune that attended their entry into Turkey clung to them at their exit, for a couple of Turkish soldiers lent as a guard by the Pasha of Buda, being sent on ahead across the Danube, were set upon and badly mauled by a party of Hungarians, one of them receiving a sword-cut across the face which nearly severed his nose.

Matters had to be explained as best they could to the local Turkish *sanjak* in the presence of the wounded man himself who appeared "with his Nose sewed together and making a lamentable Moan through it, desiring Pity for his Condition." The *sanjak* fortunately proved to be a mild tempered man and a few ducats discreetly expended served to put things right; so Busbequius and his companions passed over the river and, giving hearty thanks to Almighty God, set foot once more on Christian soil.

Two days later, at Vienna, Ferdinand received the Sultan's letter from the hand of his faithful agent, and Busbequius retired for a brief rest to recuperate from the excitements and fatigues of his eventful journeys.

CHAPTER VI

AN EMBASSY TO THE GRAND TURKE

(2)

Late in the autumn of 1554 Busbequius was invited by Ferdinand to return to Turkey with his reply to Suleyman's letter. The poor man naturally shews small enthusiasm for the mission, being convinced that he will accomplish little beyond running himself "into a Bushel of Troubles"; nor does he view with any pleasure the prospect of the weary journey in the cold and rains of December without even the element of novelty to compensate for its fatigues. He reflects, however, that, should he refuse, there is no one else to take his place and so loyally deciding "not to slip his neck from the collar" he again takes leave of his friends and sallies forth.

He once more reaches Constantinople early in January. There he finds the situation less promising than ever, for the Sultan had by now not only settled his account with the Persians but had also succeeded in quelling for a time the sporadic rebellions of his two sons, and so was free to undertake a campaign in Europe whenever he chose, without the fear of troubles breaking out behind his back. The Grand Vizir, to whom Busbequius presented himself, took pains to impress him with these facts and ominously remarked that unless he was the bearer of terms such as would satisfy the Sultan, he had far better never have come back. "Therefore, if you be wise," said he, "don't rouze a sleeping Lyon; for thereby you will but hasten your own Miseries which are coming on fast enough of themselves." Busbequius's old Turkish acquaintances also lent force to the Pasha's warning by prophesying as the mildest punishment for the Ambassador and his staff "that two of them would be cast into a Nasty Dungeon; and the third (which was to be *my* Share) would have his nose and ears cut off and so be sent back to his master."

The stout-hearted Fleming was as little deterred by these threats as by the sour looks which the common Turks cast as they passed his lodging or the coarse treatment which he received at the hands of the officials, who kept the mission penned up closely in their quarters, "less Ambassadors than Prisoners."

Suleyman, as expected, would have nothing to say to Ferdinand's proposals and after two whole years of fruitless negotiation the embassy left Constantinople to return home. Busbequius himself, however, would not accept defeat and stubbornly remained on in the Turkish capital exchanging a desultory correspondence with Vienna and hoping by his persistent importunity to bring matters to a compromise. The winter of 1558 was spent by Suleyman at Adrianople where he went with the double purpose of hawking water-fowl in the marshes and of striking further terror into the hearts of the Magyars by his nearness to their borders. Busbequius at once prepared to follow him and having obtained an escort of a dozen Janissaries from the Grand Vizir, started on the road. Of this journey he recounts an amusing little incident which may serve as a useful guide to travellers in Turkey. The roads were a morass and his guard soon began to grumble at the long marches; "their complaints," writes Busbequius "troubled me not a little, because I was loth to disoblige this sort of People, and therefore I consulted with my Servants how I might allay their Discontents and make them willinger to Travel. One of mine told me he had observed that they were much taken with a certain kind of Caudle, or Gruel which my Cook used to make of Wine, Eggs, Sugar and Spices : Perhaps (says he) if they have some of that for their Breakfast, they will become plyable. This seemed but a mean Expedient, yet we resolved to try it and the Result answered our Expectation; for after this sweet Soop away they trudged as merrily as need be and told me they would accompany me on the same terms to Buda, if I pleased."

All that Busbequius could extract from the Sultan during his stay at Adrianople was another six-months truce. Returning again to Constantinople in March he found himself more than ever a prisoner. His quarters were, it is true, in the best part of the town and commanded a distant view of Mount Olympus and of the Sea of Marmora, where he was able to watch the dolphins sporting, besides overlooking the road by which the Sultan passed from the Seraglio on his way to the *selamlik* every Friday; but there was no garden and the house was, as he puts it, "all for use and nothing for delight and pleasure." The whole lower story consisted of stables opening on a courtyard which probably accounted for the large colonies of snakes, lizards, scorpions and weasels which infested the premises. Busbequius's love for animals and his keen interest in their habits provided an excellent antidote to *ennui* and his letters contain some amusing notes on his domestic menagerie.

"For my Part," he says, "I was not content with the native Animals of the Country but filled my House with outlandish ones too; and my Family busied themselves, by my Order, to our mutual Contents in feeding them, that we might the better bear the absence from our own Country. For seeing we were debarred from human Society, what better Conversation could we have to drive Grief out of our Minds than among Wild Beasts? Otherwise Stones, Walls and Solitudes had been but lamentable Amusements for us.

"Amongst these Animals, then, Apes led the Van, which making us good Sport occasioned great Laughter amongst us, and therefore you could seldom see them without a whole Ring of my People about them delighting to observe their antick Tricks and Gestures. I also bred up some Wolves, some Bears, some broad-horned Stags (vulgarly miscalled Bucks) and common Deers; also Hinds, Lynx's, Ichneumons, or Indian Rats, and Weesels of that sort you call Ferrets and Fairies, and, if you would know all, I kept also a Hog whose noisome smell was wholesome for my Horses, as my Grooms persuaded me: So that in my nomenclature of other Creatures it is not fit I should omit my Hog which made my House to be mightily frequented by the Asiatics. They came thick and threefold to see that Creature, which is counted unclean by them, and by the Laws of their Religion they are forbid to eat it, so that they never saw one before. Yea all Turks are as afraid to touch a Hog as Christians are to come near to those who are infected with the Plague. This Humour of theirs being well known, we put a pretty Trick on them. When anyone had a mind to send me a secret Message, which he would not have my *Chiaux* know of, he put it into a little Bag together with a Roasting-Pig and sent it by a Youth. When my *Chiaux* met him, he would ask him what he had there? Then the Boy, being instructed before, whisper'd him in the Ear and said that a Friend of mine had sent me a Roasting-Pig for a Present. The *Chiaux* thereupon would punch the Bag with his Stick to see whether the Boy spake true or no; and when he heard the Pig grunt, he would run back as far as ever he could, saying 'Get thee in with the nasty Present!'; then, spitting on the Ground and turning to his Fellows, he would say ''Tis strange to see how these Christian do dote on this filthy impure Beast; they cannot forbear eating of it though their Lives were at stake.' Thus he was handsomely choused, and the Boy brought me what secret Message was sent me.

"I kept also a great many sorts of Birds, as Eagles, Jackdaws, Muscovy Ducks, Balearick Cranes and Part-ridges; yea, my House was so full of them that, if a Painter were to draw it, he may take from thence a copy of Noah's Ark.

"If you please to hear me, I'll tell you a story of a Bird : I have, among my other birds, a Balearic Crane which differs from the ordinary sort of Cranes by a white Plume of Feathers that grows hanging down from both her Ears; and besides, all the Fore-part of her Neck-Feathers were black, and the Turks adorn their Turbants with it; and there is some difference in their Bigness. This Balearic Bird was mightily affected with a Spanish Soldier, whom I had redeemed out of his Chains; when he walked abroad, the Bird would walk with him, though for many hours together; when he stood still so did the Crane; when he sat down she

would stand by him and suffer him to handle her and
stroke down her feathers, whereas she would not suffer
any body else so much as to touch her; whenever he
was gone from Home, she would come to his Chamber
Door and knock against it with her Beak; if any body
open'd it, she would look all about, to see whether he
were in the Room; and not finding him she would
traverse it about, making such a shrill Din and Noise,
that nothing living could endure it; so that we were
forced to shut her up that her Noise might not offend
us. But when he returned as soon as ever she fixed
her eyes on him, she would make to him, clapping her
wings with such an antick Posture of her Body as
Dancers in a Jig use to do; or if she had been to prepare herself for Combat with a Pigmy. In fine, she at
last used to lie under his Bed at Night, where she laid
him an Egg.

"I must tell you I have Partridges too (to acquaint
you with my whole stock of pleasurable Recreations).
You would wonder, as I did myself at first, how tame
they are. They were brought from Chios with red Feet
and Beaks. They were so troublesome to me by standing
at my Feet and picking the Dust out of my Velvet
Pantoufle with their Beaks, that they might dust themselves therewith that, to be rid of the Molestation, I was
forced to shut them up in a Chamber where in a short
time they grew over-fat and died.

"Be pleased to know that I have also a breed of
fine Horses, some of them from Syria, others from
Cicilia, Arabia and Cappodocia.

"As I take Pleasure in my Horses on other Accounts,
so especially in the Evening when I behold them brought,
one by one, out of their Stables and placed in the Yard,

6—2

that so they may enjoy the Night-Air in Summer-time and rest more sweetly. They march out so stately, shaking their Manes on their high Necks, as if they were proud to be seen, and they have fetters on their Fore-feet and one of their Hinder-feet is tied by a Cord to a Stake.

"There is no Creature so gentle as a Turkish Horse, nor more respectful to his Master or the Groom that dresses him. The reason is because they treat their Horses with great Lenity. They will with their Teeth take up a Staff or Club upon the Road, which their Rider hath let fall, and hold it up to him again ; and when they are perfect in this Lesson, then, for their Credit, they have Rings of Silver hung from their Nostrils as a Badge of Honour and good Discipline. I saw some Horses, when their Master was fallen from the Saddle, that would stand Stock-still, without wagging a Foot, until he got up again. Once too I saw some Horses, when their Master was at Dinner with me in an upper Room, prick up their Ears to hear his Voice; and when they did so, they neighed for Joy."

In the middle of the sixteenth century the possibility of another invasion of the Barbarians must have been very present in men's minds. The Turk's insatiable lust for conquest had for a generation past wrought havoc in three Continents and now, at the zenith of his power, he threatened to break loose upon Europe as his forerunners from the steppes of Asia had done eleven hundred years before. On this subject Busbequius writes in a despondent tone. After dwelling on the high efficiency of the Turkish army, the abstemiousness and hardihood of their troops, the admirable organization of their auxiliary services (such a striking contrast to the happy-go-lucky methods of European armies of that time) and the unwavering discipline of the men, he exclaims: "Thus the Turks surmount great Difficulties in War with a great deal of Patience and Sobriety. But our Christian Soldiers carry it far otherwise; they scorn homely Fare in their Camps; they must have dainty Bits, forsooth, such as Thrushes, Blackbirds and Banquetting Stuff. If they have not these, they are ready to mutiny, as if they were famished; and if they have them, they are undone—their own Intemperance kills them, if the Enemy spares their Lives.

"When I compare the Difference between their Soldiers and ours, I stand amazed to think what will be the Event; for certainly their Soldiers must needs conquer and ours be vanquished, both cannot prosperously stand together: For on their side there is a mighty, strong and wealthy Empire, great Armies, Experience in War, a veteran Soldiery, a long Series of Victories, Patience in Toil, Concord, Order, Discipline, Frugality, and Vigilance. On our Side there is public Want, private Luxury, Strength weakened, Minds discouraged, an Unaccustomedness to Labour and Arms, Soldiers refractory, Commanders covetous, a Contempt of Discipline, Licentiousness, Rashness, Drunkenness, Gluttony; and, what is worst of all, they are used to conquer, we to be conquered. Can any Man doubt in this case what the Event will be?"

In the following year, in spite of Busbequius's forebodings, the tide of War turned slightly in favour of Christian arms. A large Turkish force was repulsed in an attempt to storm Szigeth—the city before whose walls Suleyman was destined to breathe his last ten years later. This success did much to restore the spirits of the imprisoned ambassador. He had now for more than four years been cooped up in his house with a *Chaoush*, or sentry, constantly on guard at his door, who only allowed him out on the rarest occasions. The Sultan's action in treating an ambassador in this shameful manner was, as Busbequius himself admits, prompted by motives of policy. Some time before the Republic of Venice, Turkey's chief maritime rival, had sent their Agent to Constantinople to treat about the town of Napoli di Romania, lately recovered by the Venetians. The Agent was given secret instructions to try every means in his power to save the place from being handed back to the Turks, but, if it became clear that war could be averted by no other means, to offer its surrender in the last resort. A traitor having obtained a copy of these instructions, sold them to the Grand Vizir. When therefore the hapless Agent began the negotiations by swearing that the surrender of the town was not a matter for discussion, being quite outside his competence, he was at once confronted with the stolen paper and, being unable to dispute the authenticity of the document, had no choice but to sign away the town to the Turks. This incident had convinced Suleyman that Christian ambassadors usually possessed wider discretionary powers than they were willing to admit, and he hoped, by making life sufficiently intolerable for the unfortunate Busbequius, to induce him to accept the Turkish terms for peace.

It happened that just at this time a messenger, one Philip Baldus, arrived at Constantinople with despatches for Busbequius from Vienna. Rustam, the Grand Vizir, noted Baldus's arrival and drew his own conclusions from the event, supposing that he carried orders from Ferdinand to his ambassador to abate his terms.

THE GRAND VIZIR

From Rycaut's *History of the Turks*, 1669

This seemed the moment for clinching the matter by means of a veiled threat, so, on a very hot day, he sent to Busbequius a large water-melon of the sort which possesses a brilliant red core. The significance of the gift did not escape Busbequius, who knew that, according to the elaborate symbolism current among the Turks, it was equivalent to a threat of war. Any possible ambiguity was removed by the message accompanying the melon which was to the effect that the Grand Vizir advised Busbequius to use the fruit as it was suited to the season, "being an excellent Cooler"; to which Rustam added that it might interest the ambassador to know that melons of a similar sort but of much greater size grew in great quantities about Buda and Belgrade —by which he meant cannon-balls. Busbequius responded by thanking the Pasha for his gift which he promised to use, but he wished to point out that, as for the melons at Buda and Belgrade, it was no great wonder that they should grow so well there seeing that plenty of even larger dimensions flourished at Vienna. "It was a Pleasure to me," he adds in his letter, "to let Rustam know that I could retort Quibble for Quibble!"

By mid-summer of 1559 a fresh revolt by the Sultan's son Bayezid forced his father to lead the army once again into Asia. The departure of Suleyman and his troops from the capital afforded a spectacle which Busbequius decided on no account to miss. This gave rise to a humorous situation which he shall describe in his own words:

"When I was certainly informed that the Sultan was ready to pass over into Asia and that the Day was fixed for his Departure, I told my *Chiaux* that I had a mind to see him march out, and therefore he should

come betimes in the Morning and open the Doors, for
he used to carry the Keys home with him at Night.
He promised me courteously he would do so. Then
I ordered my Janissaries and my Interpreters to take
me an upper Room in the Way the Emperor was to
pass, convenient for my View, they obeyed my Commands. When the Day was come, I rose before t'was
Light expecting that the *Chiaux* had opened my Doors,
but finding them shut, I sent several Messengers to
him to come and let me out, both my Janissaries that
waited within and my Druggermen that waited without;
this I did through the chinks of the Door, which was
very old. But the *Chiaux* still spun Delays, pretending
that he would come presently. Thus I spent some time,
till I heard the Noise of the Guns, which their Emperor
used to fire when the Emperor took Horse; then I
began to fret and fume, seeing myself so deluded. My
disappointment and just Indignation did affect the Janissaries themselves; they told me that if my People would
thrust hard with them, they without would so press upon
the Valves, which were old and loose, that the Bars
would fall out. I took their Council; the Doors flew
open accordingly and out we went, hastening to the
Room I had hired.

"My *Chiaux* had a mind to frustrate my Desire,
and yet he was no bad Man either; but having com-
municated my Request to the *Bashaws*, they were not
willing that any Christian should behold their Prince
marching with so small a Force against his own Son,
'and therefore,' said they to him, 'do you promise him
fair, but be sure to delay him until the Sultan is on
Shipboard'."

"When I came to the House where a Room was

engaged for me, the Door was shut so that I could no more enter into that than I could go out of my own; when I knocked, nobody answered. Hereupon the Janissaries again told me that, if I commanded them, they would either break open the Doors or get in at the Window and open them. I told them they should not break open anything, but if they would go in at the Windows, they might; they presently did so and opened the Door. When I went up Stairs, I found the House full of Jews—a whole Synagogue of them. They looked upon it as a Miracle that I should enter when the Doors were shut; but being informed of the Truth, an old grave Matron, in comely Habit, address'd herself and complain'd to me in Spanish of the Violence I had offered to her House. I told her she had done me a Wrong in not keeping her Word, and that I was not a Man to be thus deluded. She seemed dissatisfied and the time would not admit of further Discourse. In short, I was allowed one Window which on the back side looked out into the Street, and from thence with a great deal of pleasure, I saw all the Grand Procession.

"The *Gulupagi* and *Ulufagi* marched two by two; the *Selchers* one by one. The *Spahis*, that is the Grand Seignior's Horse-Guards, were distinguished by their Ranks and Troops, being about 6000, besides a great number of the Domestics of the Prime Vizir and other *Bashaws*. The Horses were set out with Silver and Trappings studded with Gold and Jewels, and the Riders clad with a Coat or Vest made of Silk Velvet, or other Cloth of Scarlet, Purple or dark Blue Colour, intermixed with Gold and Silver. Each had two Cases hanging by his Sides; one held his Bow, the other his Arrows, both of neat Babylonian Workmanship; and so was

his Buckler which he wore on his left Arm which is
proof against Arrows, Clubs and Swords. In their right
Hands they carried light Spears painted in green. Their
Scimitars were studded with Jewels and made of Steel,
and hanged down from their Saddles. Their Heads
were covered with very fine white Cotton-Linen, in the
midst whereof stood up a Tuft of Purple Silk, plaighted;
some also wore black Feathers a-top.

"After the Horse a large Body of Janissaries followed, being a-foot and seldom carrying any other Arms
than Muskets. The Make and Colour of their Clothes
are almost the same, so that you would judge them all
to be the Servants of one Man. Yet in their Feathers,
Crests and suchlike military Ornaments, they are over-
curious or rather proud, especially the veterans in the
Rear—you would think a whole Wood of walking
Feathers were in their Fire-stars and Frontals. After
them their Officers and Commanders follow on Horseback, distinguished each by his own Ensign. In the
last Place marches their *Aga* or General. Then succeed
the chief Courtiers among whom are the *Bashaws*; then
the Foot of the Prince's Life-guard in a peculiar Habit,
carrying their Bows bent in their Hands, for they are
all Archers; next the Prince's Led-Horses, all with
curious Trappings. He himself rode on a stately Prancer,
looking sour with his brows bent, as if he had been
angry; behind him came three Youths, one carrying
a Flagon of Water, another his Cloak, another his Bow.
There followed some Eunuchs of the Bed-Chamber;
and at last a Troop of about Two Hundred Horse
closed the Procession.

"After I had the Satisfaction of viewing all this,
my only Care was to appease my Hostess, I sent for

her and told her she should have remembered her Bargain and not have shut the Door against me ; 'but though you,' said I, 'don't remember your Promise, I'll perform mine; yes, I will be better than my Word : I promis'd you but seven Pistoles, but here's ten for you, that so you may not repent your Admittance of me into your House.' When the Woman thus unexpectedly saw her Hand filled with Gold, she was melted down into a Compliance, and the whole Synagogue of them fell to Compliments and giving me Thanks. They offered me Grecian Wine and a Banquet which I refused, but, with great Acclamations of all the Jews made haste to be gone that I might manage a new Dispute with my *Chiaux* for keeping my Doors fastened when I should have come forth.

"I found him sitting mournfully in my Porch, where he began a long Complaint, that I ought not to have gone abroad without his Consent, nor have broken open the Door ; that I had violated the Law of Nations thereby, and suchlike Stuff. I replied that if he had come betimes in the Morning as he had promised, he had prevented all this ; his Breach of Promise had occasioned it. I demanded also of him whether he looked upon me as an Ambassador or as a Prisoner ? 'As an Ambassador,' says he. 'If you think me a Prisoner,' said I, 'then I am not a fit Instrument to make a Peace, for a Prisoner is not his own Man, but if an Ambassador, as you confess, then why am I not a free Man ? Captives use to be shut up, not Ambassadors : Liberty is granted to such in all Nations : they may claim it as their public due : He ought to know that he was not appointed to be my Serjeant or Keeper, but to assist me with his good Offices, that so no other Man might do an Injury to me or mine.'"

Shortly after his successful conflict with his jailors, Busbequius succeeded in obtaining the Sultan's permission to visit the army encamped on the Asiatic shore. Here, being more in the public eye, he found himself far better treated ; he was freed from all the petty annoyances to which he was interminably subjected at Constantinople and was, on the contrary, provided with a handsome lodging and every facility for studying the habits and methods of a Turkish army in the field. As before, he is intensely impressed by the discipline and orderliness of the soldiers and the complete absence of rowdiness, drunkenness and gambling. His visit to the camp terminated rather abruptly after a regrettable encounter between a party of his own servants and some Janissaries. The latter returning *en deshabille* from a swim in the sea, were insulted by the embassy servants who failed to recognize them and paid handsomely for their error. For a time relations were somewhat strained between Busbequius and the Sultan, as the former, with his usual stubbornness, refused to offer any satisfaction for his men's behaviour ; there arrived however, on the scene a learned and worthy person of Amsterdam " who had been sent by Ferdinand to carry some royal presents to Suleyman (including a clock " neatly made and borne like a Tower on an Elephant's Back ") which mightily took the fancy of the Grand Seigneur and restored him to comparative good humour. So Busbequius came back again to his dismal quarters in the capital and resigned himself to a further spell of his monotonous existence, relieved only by the society of his family of pets and his encounters with the petty tyrant who acted as the guardian of his portals.

CHAPTER VII

AN EMBASSY TO THE GRAND TURKE

(3)

The year 1560 saw Busbequius' exile in Turkey drawing to its close: it also witnessed an event which
was to bring a great change into his life at the capital.
This was the arrival of the broken relics of the Christian
allied fleet defeated by the Turks off the island of Jerba
on the North African coast. Busbequius's description of
the sad spectacle of the captured ships being towed into
harbour is reserved for a later chapter, so we may
proceed at once to his account of the treatment of the
unfortunate crews.

"The Prisoners," he says "were brought into the
Seraglio, but so miserably Hunger-starv'd that some
could hardly stand on their Legs; others fell down in a
Swoon from very Feebleness; others had Arms put upon
them in a Jeer, in which Posture they died. The Turks
insulted over them on every Hand, promising to themselves the Empire of the whole World; 'for who shall
now be able to stand before us (they said) since we have
overcome the Spaniards?'"

To be captured by the Turk in those days meant,
as a rule, a lifetime of misery in the slave-galleys and
it is hard to picture adequately the utter hopelessness
which must have filled the hearts of these wretched
prisoners. A few of the higher officers avoided the
common lot. Don Bellinger, the Genoese Admiral
purchased at a great price the privilege of internment

on Chios, but the military commander-in-chief, Don
Alvarez de Sande, Duke of Medina, was shut up
in a castle on the shores of the Black Sea, while
most of the rank and file were thrust into Galata
Tower. The tragic circumstances of his fellow-Christians deeply affected Busbequius and he lost no
time and spared no effort in doing what he could to
mitigate their sufferings. He describes the work as
follows: "I was forced to provide several sorts of Relief
for their several Necessities, different Diseases requiring
different Cures. There lay a Multitude of sick Persons
in a certain Temple of Pera, whom the Turks cast out
as Abjects, and many of these perished for want of convenient Broths for their sick Stomachs. When I was
told thereof, I dealt with a Friend of mine, a Citizen of
Pera, desiring him to buy some Weather-Sheep every
day and boil them at his own House to distribute the
Flesh to some, and the Broth to others, as their Stomachs
could bear, which was a great Relief to Abundance of
them. But those that were in Health required another
sort of Assistance and my House was full from Morning
to Night with many Complaints. Some were used to
good Diet, and a Piece of brown Bread—which was
their daily Allowance—would not go down well with
them; some that used to drink Wine could not bear the
perpetual use of Water only; some wanted Blankets to
cover them, having never known what it was to lie on
the bare Ground; some wanted Coats, some Shoes, but
the most part desired some Footing-money to gratify
their Keepers, that they might deal the more mercifully
with them. Money was the only Remedy for these
Mischiefs, so that every day some Guilders were expended by me on their Account. But these Expenses
were tolerable, compared with certain greater Sums that

were desired of me for some prayed me to be their Surety
for their Ransom-Money; and herein every one was
very forward with his Pretences, one alleging Nobleness
of Birth, another that he had great Friends and Alliances,
a Third that he was Commander in the Army and had
much Pay due to him, a Fourth that he had Cash enough
at Home and was able to imburse me. Some boasted
of their Valour in the Fight, indeed every one had something to say for himself. When I demanded them
whether they were sure to repay me? 'God forbid,'
said they 'for what is more unjust than to defraud a
Man that hath restored us to our Liberty, even out of
the Jaws of Death?'

"And the Truth is it was very grievous to me to see
their State, and so I was induced to pass my Word, in
all, for 1000 Ducats and have thereby run myself so
much into Debt that I fear I have but freed them from
Fetters only to clap them on my own Legs."

Poor Busbequius was now to experience the truth of
the old adage that troubles never come singly. His
next misfortune, which, though it may not seem of
so desperate a nature to us of the present day,
was evidently a most cruel blow to him, arose from
the growing cantankerousness and fanaticism which
the Sultan developed in his old age. "Solyman,"
writes Busbequius, "grows every day more and more
superstitious in his Religion. He used to delight himself in Musicke and in the chanting of young Singers,
but all this has now been laid aside by the work of a
certain old Sibyl, noted for Sanctity, who told him, if
he left not off that Sport, he would be severely punished
after his Death. He was also prevailed upon by her to
forbid the use of Wine. Hereupon an Edict was pub-

lished that for the Future no Wine should be imported
into Constantinople, either for Christians or Jews."

For several weeks Busbequius fought his case stoutly
with the Grand Vizir and the chief Pashas, appealing
to his ambassadorial privileges and pointing out the
disastrous effects which the drinking of water was likely
to have on his health, the sudden change being calculated, he assured them, to cause serious disease, if not
death itself. At last after a supreme effort, he extracted
from the Vizir a concession which permitted him to
convey, carefully concealed in a travelling carriage, as
much wine as could be transported between dark and
dawn on a single night from the nearest landing place
to the Embassy cellars.

A far worse thing befell the mission shortly after,
when the plague got a footing in the house. Once more
Suleyman's religious bigotry was their undoing, for when
Busbequius requested leave to abandon the plague-
stricken premises, the only answer the Sultan vouch-
safed to him was: "Is not Pestilence God's Arrow, which
will always hit his Mark? If God would visit me here
how could I avoid it? Is not the Plague in my own
Palace, and yet I do not think of removing?" "And so,"
adds Busbequius, "I was forced to stay in a Pestilential
and Infected House." The Pestilence passed and the
Ambassador himself survived, but he lost his best friend
and faithful physician, the excellent Dr Quackquellen,
whom he buried with many tears in unconsecrated soil
erecting a monument over his grave "as a due testimony
to his Vertue."

All too late a capricious *volte face* on the part
of the Sultan brought permission for a change of air
and Busbequius left his dismal quarters in Stamboul for

a villa on the pleasant island of Prinkipo[1], one of the little group situated a few miles distant from Constantinople in the Sea of Marmora. Here Busbequius spent three months enjoying himself as he had never done since he arrived in Turkey seven years before. The island was inhabited solely by Greek fishermen and the genial Ambassador joined with zest in their usual avocation. "The Sea" he writes, "is full of divers sorts of Fishes, which I took sometimes with Net, sometimes with Hook and Line. Several Grecian Fishers with their boats attended me and where we had hopes of the greatest sport thither we sailed and cast our Nets. Sometimes we played above board and when we saw a Crab or a Lobster at the bottom, where the Sea was very clear, we ran him through with a Fishspear, and so halled him up into a Vessel. But our best and most profitable sport was with a drag-net; where we thought most fish were there we cast it in a round; it took up a great compass, with the ropes tied to the end of it, which were to bring it to Land. To those Ropes the Fisher tied green Boughs very thick, so that the Fish might be frightned, and not seek to escape. Thus we brought great Sholes of trembling Fishes to Shore. Sea-Bream, Scorpion-Fishes, Dragon-Fishes, Scare-Fish, Jule-Fish, Chane or Ruff-Fish, whose variety did delight my eye and the inquiry into their nature did hugely please my Fancy.

"When tempestuous Weather kept me from the Sea," he continues, "I delighted myself in finding out strange and unusual Plants at Land. I would sometimes go afoot all over the Island, having a young Franciscan

[1] The home of another illustrious State prisoner in the person of General Townshend, the defender of Kut.

Monk in my Company, a jolly Fellow, but very fat, and not used to travel on Foot. I took him out of a Monastry at Pera, to be my Partner in my Walks; he was so corpulent and pursy, that when I went on a-pace to catch myself a Heat, he would follow me at a Distance panting and blowing, with these words in his Mouth, 'What need all this haste? Whom do we run from, or whom do we pursue? What are we carriers or Posts that must make speed to deliver some important Letters?' thus he mutter'd, till the very Sweat pierced through all his Cloaths. In fine, when we came back to our Lodging, he threw himself upon his Bed, wofully complaining, and crying out, he was undone: 'What Injury have I done, said he, that you thus hurry on to destroy me?' And, in this fretting Posture, we had much ado to persuade him to eat a bit of Dinner."

On the subject of monks Busbequius tells the following story of a scene which took place after his return to the capital. "Let me now tell you" he says "a wondrous Story of a wandering Turkish Monk. He wore a Cap and white Cloak down to his Heels, with long hair such as Painters draw the Apostles with. He had a promising Countenance, but was a meer Impostor; and yet the Turks admired him as a Miraculous Man. My Interpreters were persuaded to bring him to me that I might see him. He dined with me soberly and modestly enough; afterwards he goes down into the Yard, and upon his return he takes up a huge Stone and struck with it divers times upon his naked Breast as many blows as would have felled an Ox: Then he took a piece of Iron that was heated in the Fire on purpose, and thrust it into his Mouth, where he stirred it up and down so that his Spittle hiss'd again; 'twas a long piece of Iron, thick and quadrangular in that part which he thrust into his Mouth and it was red-hot as a live Coal: Then he put the Iron into the Fire again, and after I had made him a Present, he saluted me and departed. My Domesticks wonder'd at the Trick, all but one who pretended that he knew more than all the rest; Oh, says he, he is a meer Cheat; and thereupon he takes hold of the stronger part of the Iron, pretending he could do as much as the Juggler. He had no sooner grasped it in his Hands than he threw it away, and his Fingers were well burnt for his Audaciousness, so that they were many days acuring. This accident caused his fellows to laugh, and jearingly to ask whether the Iron were hot enough yet, and whether he would touch it again or not.

"The same Turk, while he was at Dinner, told me that the Prior of their Monastery was a Man famous for sanctity and Miracles, for he would spread his Cloak over a Lake near adjoining and sitting on it, would row up and down whithër he pleased: And that he would strip himself naked, and be tied to a Sheep newly kill'd tying arms to arms, and Leg to Leg and so would be thrown into the hot Oven till the Sheep were bak'd fit to be eaten, then he himself would be taken out without any harm at all: You will not believe this; neither do I, only I relate what he told me; but that part concerning the red-hot Iron I saw with my own eyes."

Wandering on from one subject to another in his pleasant discoursive way Busbequius entertains the friend to whom he addresses his letters with a disquisition on Turkish table manners and mentions the custom among guests at a dinner-party of taking tit-bits home with them for their women-folk. "Let me tell you" he adds, "a Story to this purpose, which I know will make you laugh heartily, as it did me at the first hearing it. 'Tis the custom of the Turkish Bashaws, some days before their Fast to make a public Feast or Entertainment for all Comings; none are excluded, yet generally none but Servants, Friends and Relations come. There is a Napkin made of Leather spread over a long Tapestry on the Ground, full of Dishes; the Table will hold abundance of Guests; the Bashaw himself sits at the upper End and the choicest Guests next to him, and then the ordinary Guests in ranks, till the Table be full. It will not hold all at once, but some stand by till the others have din'd, which they do with great Decency and Silence; and then drinking a Draught of Honey diluted with Water, salute their Landlord and away they go. In their Places others sit down, and the third Class after them; the Servants still taking off the old Dishes and setting on new. A certain Bashaw, making such a Feast, invited a *Sanziack* to sit next to him; an old Man of the Sect the Turks call *Hojies,* that is learned Men, sat next to him, This *Hoji,* seeing such Plenty of Victuals before him, had a Mind to carry home some to his Wife after he had filled his own Belly; but looking for his Handkerchief to fill it with Victuals, he found he had left it at home; being then in a straight, he bethought himself and resolv'd to fill his Sleeve which hanged on his Back, but mistaking the *Sanziack's* for his own, he stuft it full of Dainties and stops it in with a Piece of Bread that nothing might fall out. He was not to touch his Sleeve till he had lay'd his Hands on his Breast or Thigh and so saluted his Entertainer, as their Custom is; when he had done that he took up his own Sleeve and finds it empty, at which he was much amazed and returned home very sad. A while after the *Sanziack*

A *HOJA*

From Rycaut's *History of the Turks*, 1669

also rose from the Table and, having saluted the Bashaw at every Step, his Sleeve cast out the Dainties it was replenished with unknown to him, and seeing a Train of Junkets behind him, he blushed for Shame. The Company fell a laughing, but the Bashaw imagining how it came to pass, desired him to sit down again, and sent for the *Hoji*; when he came, he accosted him thus: 'I wonder that you, an old Friend, and having a Wife and Children at home, did carry home nothing to them, seeing my Table was so well furnished.' 'Truly, Sir,' said he, ''twas no Fault of mine, but of my Evil Genius; for I stuffed my Sleeve with Viands and yet when I came out I found it empty.' Thus the *Sanziack* was cleared and the Disappointment of the *Hoji*, together with the Novelty of the Case occasioned no small Laughter throughout all the Company."

Busbequius's indomitable patience bore fruit at last. He had indeed, after the recent Christian reverses, to "draw in his Sails somewhat"—as he quaintly phrases it—but a formula for a treaty was eventually agreed upon between him and the Grand Vizir which satisfied Suleyman and was approved in principle by the Emperor. Busbequius's powers permitted of his signing the treaty on behalf of Ferdinand, "but," said he "I knew there want not Sycophants in Princes' Courts who go about to obscure the best Services of their Ministers, especially if Strangers. I therefore thought it fit to leave all to the Pleasure of my Master." So he cautiously represented to the Turks that certain of the treaty articles were obscure and that, though confident of the Emperor's acceptance, he would prefer to travel to Vienna accompanied by an Agent of the Porte who could explain their interpretation and obtain Ferdinand's own signature. To this the Grand Vizir assented, and appointed the Drago-man of the Porte, a certain Ibrahim, to be their Agent.

When the time for his departure came, Busbequius was invited by the Divan to the customary banquet given to an ambassador on the termination of his mission. Adhering to his policy of leaving open the door to the last moment, he refused the feast, though gladly accepting a queerly assorted gift from his old friend, the Grand Vizir, consisting of three excellent Arabian horses, together with a waistcoat embroidered in gold, a glass of rare balsam and a box of Alexandrian treacle, "the best in the World." The Sultan, surly to the last, gave him none but the common gifts bestowed on petty envoys and an ill-tempered homily on the futility of opposing his imperial will.

Shortly before Busbequius had, by his unwearying efforts, succeeded in obtaining the release of Don Al-varez de Sande, the ill-starred general captured at the fall of Jerba, and the grateful Spaniard accompanied his benefactor on the journey home. De Sande was such a man as Busbequius loved, a cheerful, facetious fellow with a fund of anecdote and a nature as boyish as the Ambassador's own. They found each other excellent company capping one another's stories and running races on the road "in which", says Busbequius, " I, being lean, could easily out pace him who was fat and pursy and just out of Prison." Ibrahim, possessed with oriental notions of propriety, regarded with horror these undig-nified performances on the part of the travelling com-panions "and beseeched us, by all that we held dear, not to be seen on foot by the Villages for it would be accounted a Disgrace to us among the Turks." His implorings sometimes availed to induce the pair back into their coach but often "the Pleasure of walking afoot still got the better."

The inevitable *contretemps* near the frontier duly repeated itself and again the Ambassador and his company got into serious trouble at the moment of leaving Ottoman territory. A doctor and a Spaniard belonging to the party accompanied by some of the guards were searching for lodgings for the night and came to the house of a local Janissary. "Hereupon the Janissary, Master of the House, being told that some Christian passengers were seeking for a Lodging at his House : came in a great Rage with a Club like Hercules's in his Hand, and without speaking a Word, strikes the Physician a great Blow on the Shoulders as hard as he was able ; the Physician, to avoid a second Blow, ran out of the House. My Servant looking back saw him lift up his Club to strike him also : but he, having a thing like a Hatchet in his Hand held it crossways over his Head, and so kept off many a lusty Blow, till at last the Handle of the Hatchet, by his often striking, began to break. Then my Servant was forced to close with the Janizary, and was about to cleave his Skull with his Weapon : Whereupon the Janizary fled and my Servant not being able to overtake him, threw the Hatchet after him, which cut him in the Hams and fell'd him to the Ground ; by which Accident my People escaped. On hearing what had taken place de Sande was tormented lest he should be carried back to Constantinople. He was much offended with my Servant who had wounded the Janizary, especially for saying that he was very sorry he had not killed him on the Spot. His Words to him were these : 'Honest Henry, Prithee be not so Passionate ; 'tis no Time or Place to shew thy Valour here ; We

must bear Affronts patiently, without any just Imputa-
tion of Cowardice whether we will or no ; we are in
their Power : This unreasonable Passion may bring
great Mischief to us : perhaps it may occasion us to be
brought back to Constantinople, and there our whole
Negotiation may be reversed or at least become very
dubious. I beseech Thee, therefore, for my Sake among
the rest, govern thy Passion.'

"But Henry was deaf to all his Persuasions; he being
an obstinate Fellow and when angry would not hearken
to Reason. 'What care I,' replied he, 'if I had killed him?
Did he not design to kill me? If one of his many Blows
had gone home he had knock'd me down like an Ox.
Were I to be blamed if I slew him who would have
slain me first ? I am sorry with all my heart I did not
give him his Death's Wound. But for the Future (take
my Word for it) I'll spare never a Turk of them all; for
if he assaults me I'll give him as good as he brings,
though it cost me my Life.'"

In this dilemma recourse was had to Ibrahim who
saved the awkward situation in which "honest Henry"
had landed his masters by interviewing the injured
Janissary in bed and persuading him that any further
interference with a gentleman who stood in such favour
with the Sultan as Busbequius would inevitably cost
him his head. This bold threat "took down my Janizary's
crest," Busbequius remarks, "and put him into a terrible
Panick besides," and so the incident was happily closed.

Two days later, to the intense relief of de Sande,
who doubted his safety till he was actually across the
boundary, Busbequius's party found themselves on
Austrian soil.

At Vienna they learnt that the Emperor Ferdinand,

who had now succeeded Charles V as Emperor, was at Frankfort attending the Imperial Diet where the preliminaries were being arranged for the crowning of his son Maximilian as King of the Romans. After an interchange of letters with Ferdinand the party continued their journey to Frankfort where Busbequius was received by his master "with all imaginable kindness" and made his report of the results of his mission. The gates of the town which were by ancient usage shut on the eve of the assembly of the Diet were opened by express command for the Turkish envoy and he was given a special place at the procession from which to see—and be duly impressed by—"the glorious and magnificent Sight of so many Christian Princes in perfect Unanimity passing by with great Pomp and Splendor." A few days later the Emperor received Ibrahim and formally confirmed the seven years' treaty of peace which had been secured by the courage and untiring devotion of his faithful ambassador during his seven years of exile at the court of the Grand Signior.

CHAPTER VIII

TWO MARTIAL ADVENTURES

(1)

A stroller prying among the bookshops of St Paul's Churchyard in the early part of the seventeenth century might have had his eye arrested at the Sign of the Green Dragon by a couple of recent publications describing adventures in Turkey, one a fat little duodecimo entitled *Voyages in the Levant by Hy. Blunt, Gent.*, the other a mere pamphlet headed "Newes from Turkie by a Gentleman of Qualitie." The former describes a journey through the Balkans in the train of a Turkish Army marching to the wars; the latter consists of the diary of a volunteer who fought in the Polish army against the Turks in Bessarabia. Both of the authors are entertaining writers and between them they give an excellent picture of the Turk in warfare, so their narratives well deserve a place in these pages. We will take the *Voyages* first.

Henry Blunt was a globe trotter with a strong philosophical bias and is careful to explain the motives which urged him to a tour of Turkey. The knowledge of human affairs, says he, " which formeth the strongest desire of intellectual complexions " is best advanced by the study of peoples who differ most greatly from our own. It is natural, he continues, that inhabitants of the North-West part of the globe should meet with their opposite extremes among the peoples who live in the South-East corner. Given these premisses he argues that an English philosopher should find the fullest scope for research in observing the customs of the Turks.

He adds to this excellent syllogism another good reason for his decision to travel in Turkey. "The Turke," he says, "being the only modern people great in action, whose Empire hath invaded the world and fixt itselfe such firm foundations as no other ever did, I was of opinion that he who would beholde the present times in their greatest glory could not find a better scene than Turkie."

With these commendable objects in view Blunt set forth on his travels. Let us overtake him at Venice where he is making his final arrangements for the journey and looking for a ship to take him down the east coast of the Adriatic, at that time a notable bone of contention between the Venetians and the Turks.

"First," he writes, "I agreed with a janizary to find me Dyet, Horse, Coach, Passage and all other usual charges as farre as a Venetian Gally with a Caravan of Turks and Jewes bound for the Levant, not having any Christians with them beside myself; this occasion was right to my purpose, for familiarity of bed, board and passage together is more opportune to disclose the customes of men than a much longer habitation in Cities, where society is not so linked and behaviour is more personate than in travell.

"The Gally lying that day and night at Lido, set saile the next morn and in four and twenty houres arrived at Rovinio, a Venetian city in Istria; from thence wee came to Zara, which city stands in Dalmatia and of all others within the Gulfe is, by reason of its situation, most apt to command the whole Adriatique and therefore hath formerly been attempted by the Turke, wherefore the Venetians have fortified it extraordinarily and now, though in times of firm peace, keep it with strong companies of Horse and Foot. After a day's view of this place wee sailed to Spalatro, a city of Sclavonia, kept by the Venetians as their only Emporium there, being plyed successively with two Gallies which carry between Venice and that place such merchandize as is transported into Turky, or from thence brought in. It stands in a most pleasant valley on the South side of great mountaines, and in the wall towards the sea there appears a great remainder of a gallery in Diocletian's Palace. In this Towne the Venetians allow the great Turk to take custome of the Merchandize whereupon there resides his Emir, or Treasurer."

At Spalato the caravan landed and after resting three days took the road across the Dinaric Alps to Serajevo, or as the Turks still call it, Bosna Serai. But let Blunt describe the journey in his own words.

"The first journey wee began about Sunset, our lodging two miles off wee pitched upon a little hill grown over with Juniper, once the seat of Salonae, famous for their bravery against Octavius, there is now not so much as a ruine left excepting a piece of Diocletian's Aqueduct. Hence wee passed the Hills of Dogliana, far higher then the Alps and so steep was our descent for three days together that it was a greater precipice than that coming downe from Mont Cenis into Piemont. Having rode thus for nine days, wee came into a spacious and fruitful plaine which at the West, where wee entered, is at least ten miles over, but at the North and South immured with ridges of easie and pleasant hills till, by degrees, after six or seven miles riding it grows not above a mile broad. There found wee the city Saraih which extends from the one side to the other and takes up part of both Ascents. At the East end stands a Castle upon a steep rock commanding the town and the passage Eastward.

"This is the Metropolis of the Kingdome of Bosnah: it is but meanly built and not great, reckoning about fourscore Mescheetoes[1] and twenty thousand houses."

It was here that Blunt and his companions fell in with the Turkish army. The Sultan at that time was Murad IV, a despot of fierce, relentless temper and almost fiendish cruelty who used to exercise the royal prerogative of taking ten innocent lives a day by sitting in his palace on the Bosphorus and practising "pot-shots" in archery on any luckless passer-by. With these unpleasant attributes he combined a real genius for leadership and organization and succeeded in averting the dangerous anarchy which had set in under his immediate predecessors and in making the Turkish armies more formidable than ever to his Christian neighbours.

At the moment of Blunt's arrival in Turkey Murad was designing the invasion of Poland and orders had gone forth to the Pashas all over the empire to assemble with their troops at the rendezvous at Belgrade. The local contingent was starting just as the caravan reached Serajevo and, for the sake of safety, they joined themselves to it. It is to this accident that we are indebted for Blunt's admirable description of an army on the march.

[1] Scil. mosques—"mescheetoes" representing a half-way stage in the evolution of the word from the arabic *masjid*, a place-of-adoration.

"At our departure," he says, "wee went along with the Bashaw of Bosnah's troopes going for the Warre of Poland, they were of Horse and Foot between six and seven thousand, but went scattering. The Bashaw was not yet in person, and the taking leave of their friends spirited many of them with drinke and made them fitter company for the Devill than for a Christian. Myself, after many launces and knives threatened upon mee, was invaded by a drunken Janizary whose iron Mace entangling in his other furniture gave mee time to flee among the rocks and so escape untouched.

"Thus marched we ten days through a hilly country, cold, uninhabited and in a manner a continuous wood, mostly of Pine trees; at length we reached Valliovah, a pretty little Towne upon the confines of Hungary where the Camp staying some days, wee left them behind. Having to pass a wood near the Christian country and doubting it to be (as confines are) full of Thieves, wee divided our Caravan of sixscore Horse into two parts: half with the persons and goods of least esteem we sent on a day before the rest, so that the Thieves having a booty might be gone before wee came—which happened accordingly. They were robbed and one thief and two of our men slain, with some hundred Dollars worth of goods lost. The next day wee ourselves passed and found sixteen Theeves in a narrow passage, before whom wee set a good guard of Harquebuse and Pistolls till the weaker sort passed by; so in three days wee came safe to Belgrada."

Belgrade was not at this period the great outpost of the Turkish Empire which it subsequently became and still was in the early part of last century when Kinglake wrote his grim account of the Styx-like crossing from Semlin to the plague-stricken portal of the Sultan's dominions. A hundred years and more before Blunt's time the town had fallen to Suleyman's armies which swept beyond and established the frontier far to the North; but already in those days the huge bluff which rises wedge-shaped in the angle where the Save and Danube meet was topped by the forbidding fortress which was often to check the Christian invader in the later days of Turkey's weakness. The town and castle are thus described by Blunt.

"The City stands most in a bottom encompassed Eastward by gentle and pleasant ascents, employed in Orchards and Vines; Southward is an easie Hill, part possessed with buildings and the rest a burial-place well nigh three miles in compass so full of graves as one can bee by another. The West end yields a right magnificent aspect by reason of an eminency of land jetting out farther than the rest and bearing a goodly strong Castle whose walls are two miles about, fortified with a dry ditch and out-works.

"This Castle on the West side is washed by the great river Sava, which on the North side of the City loses itself in the Danubius, held to be the greatest river in the World.

"The Castle is excellently furnished with Artillery, and at the entrance there stands an Arsenal with some forty or fifty fair Brasse peeces, most bearing the Armes and inscription of Ferdinand the Emperour. That which to mee seemed strangest in this Castle (for I had liberty to pry up and downe) was a round Tower, called the Zindana, a cruelty not devised by the Turks and by them seldom practised[1]. This Tower is large and

---

[1] This was the "gauch," a pretty common instrument of death among the Turks at that time despite Blunt's statement to the contrary.

round, but severed within into many squares with long
beams set on end about four foot asunder; each beam
was stuck frequent with great flesh-hookes and the
person condemned was let fall thereon, which gave him
a quick or lasting misery as he chanced to light: then
at the bottom the river is let in by grates, whereby the
corpses are washt away.

"Within this great Castle is another little one with
works of its own. I had like to have miscarried with
approaching its entrance, had not the rude noise and
worse lookes of the guard given mee a timely appre-
hension to sweeten them with sudden passage and
humiliation and so get off; for, as I learnt after, there
is a great part of the Grand Signior's treasure kept
there to be ready when he warres on that side the
Empire, and it is death for any Turk or Christian to
enter."

The troops in whose company Blunt was travelling
had their rendezvous at Belgrade with the contingents
from Temesvar and Buda, and here the various Pashas
assembled with their followings of *spahis*, janissaries
and *akinjis*, while awaiting the arrival of the Grand Vizir
who was marching from the Capital at the head of
four thousand Timariots.

As soon as the Grand Vizir reached Belgrade the
whole army, our friend with them, started for Sofia,
twelve days distant. Blunt gives a very graphic picture
of the march of this large force. "The Bashaes," he
says, "did not all goe in company, but setting forth
about an houre one after the other, drew out their
troopes in length without confusion; yet not in much
order of Ranke and File, as being near no ememy. In
this and our former march I much admired that our

Caravan loaded with Cloths, Silkes and Tissues and other rich commodities remained so safe not only in the main Army but also among straggling troopes, where we often wandered by reason of the need to recover the Jewes' Sabboth. But I found the cause to be the cruelty of Justice, for Theeves upon the way are empaled without delay; and there was also a Sanjacke with two hundred Horse who did nothing but coast up and down the country and every man who could not give a fair account of his being where he found him was presently strangled even though not known to have offended."

It was by such drastic measures as these that Sultan Murad had succeeded in restoring the iron discipline of the Ottoman army which had lapsed into licence under the feeble successors of the great Suleyman. Judged by the standards of the day, when European armies were only just emerging from the condition of armed rabbles, the Turkish armies were a model of organization.

"It was a wonder," says Blunt, "to see such a multitude of men clear of confusion, violence, want, sicknesse or any other disorder; for, though wee were almost threescore thousand and sometimes found not a Town in seven or eight days, yet there was such a plenty of good Bisket, Rice and Mutton that wheresoever I passed up and down to view the Spahyes and others in their tents, they would often make mee sit and eat with them very plentifully and well."

But while the old Turkish traditions of hardiness and discipline were more or less rigidly maintained in the ranks, there was a very different state of affairs among the commanders, who had forsaken the stern simplicity of earlier days for a truly Byzantine *régime* of luxury. Not even on active service would the beys and pashas willingly abandon the habits of luxury which were already sapping the pristine energy of the race. Their decadent manners did not escape the observant eye of the Englishman travelling in their train, who thus describes the routine of their camp life.

"The severall Courts of the Bashaes were served in great state each of them having three or fourscore camels, besides six or seven score carts to carry the Baggage; and when the Basha himself took horse he had five or six Coaches covered with cloth of gold or rich tapestrie to carry his wives, of whom some had with them twelve or sixteen, the least ten. When these entered the Coach, there were men set on either side holding up a rowe of tapestrie to cover them from being seen by the people, although they were, after the Turkish manner, muffled that nothing but the eye could appear. Besides these wives each Basha had as many, or likely more, Catamites, which are their serious loves: for their wives are used (as the Turks themselves told me) but to dress their meat, to laundresse, and for reputation. The boys of twelve or fourteen yeares old, some of them not above nine, are usually clad in velvet or scarlet with gilt Scymitars, and are bravely mounted with sumptious furniture: to each of them a Souldier appointed who walks by his bridle for his safety.

"When they are all in order there is excellent Sherbets given to whoever will drink; then the Basha takes horse, before whom ride a dozen or more, who with ugly drums, brasse Dishes and wind instruments noise along most part of the journey. Before all goe Officers to pitch his tent where he shall lodge or dine. When meat is served up, especially at night, all the people give three great Shouts."

It is not surprising that a solitary Englishman travelling in such company should meet with strange experiences and two adventures which befell Blunt are well worth repeating. "That," he says, "which secured and emboldened my passage these twelve days march was an accident the first night, which was as follows: the Campe being pitched by the shoare of Danubius, I went (but timorously) to view the service about Murad Basha's Court, where one of his favorite boyes espying mee to be a stranger gave mee a cup of Sherbet. I in thankes, and to make friends at Court, presented him with a Pocket Looking glasse in a little ivory case with a combe, such as are sold at Westminster Hall at four or five shillings a-piece. The youth, much taken therewith, ran and shewed it to the Bashaw, who presently sent for mee and making me sit and drink Cauphe in his presence, called for one that spake Italian and demanded of my condition, purpose, countrey and many other particulars. It was my fortune to hit his humour so right that at last he asked mee if my Law did permit me to serve under them against the Polacke, who is a Christian, promising with his hand on his breast that, if I would, I should be enrolled of his Companies, furnished with a good horse and, for other necessaries be provided like the rest of his household. I humbly thanked him for his favour and told him that to an Englishman it was lawful to serve under any who were in league with our King, and that our King had not only a league with the Gran Signior, but continually held an ambassadoure at his Court, esteeming him the greatest Monarch in the World, so that my service, especially if I behaved myself not unworthy of my Nation, would be exceedingly well received in England. I added that the Polacke, though in name a Christian, was yet of a sect that for Idolatry and many other points wee abhorred, wherefore the English had of late helped the Muscovite against him and wee would be forwarder under the Turks, whom we not only honoured for their glorious actions in the world but also loved for the kind commerce of Trade which we find amongst them. But as for my present engagement to the War, with much sorrow I acknowledged my incapacity by reason I wanted language, which would not only render mee incapable of command and so unserviceable, but also endanger mee in tumults, where I appearing a stranger and not able to express my affection might be mistaken and used harshly. For such reasons I humbly entreated his Highnesse leave to follow my own poor affaires with an eternal oblige to blazon this honourable favour wheresoever I came.

" He forthwith bad mee do as liked me best, wherewith I took my leave. But such confidence had I in his favour that I went often to observe his Court."

The other and far more alarming adventure happened when the caravan had halted at Nish to allow the Jews of the party to observe their sabbath.

"A little before night," says Blunt, " Wine having possessed a Janizary and one other Turke who rode in my Coach, they fell out with two country fellowes and by violence took an Axe from one of them, not to rob him but for present use thereof; which being done I gave him his axe again as not willing in these parts to have so much as an observer's part in a quarrel. These fellowes dogg'd us: the Janizary they missed, but at midnight came to our Coach where wee slept and opened the cover. Whereat I speaking in Italian they knew me, wherefore leaving me, they drew the Turke by the neck and shoulders and gave him two blows with a Scymitar, one over the arm, the other upon the head, in such sort that they left him behind in great danger of death. They then fled and I was found there all bloody and, so taken, had surely the next day been executed but that within lesse than halfe an houre the hurt person coming to his senses cleared mee, telling how the matter came and by whom."

In due course Blunt and his fellow travellers arrived at "Sophya, the chieffe City of Bulgary," where the local characteristic which most impressed him was the diminutive size of the doors of the houses which, he says, "are little above three feet high, which they told me was that the Turkes might not bring their Horses, who else would use them for stables in their travels; which I noted for a greater sign of slavery than in other places."

Much to his own disappointment, and equally to his readers' loss, Blunt was forced to part company with the Turkish army on reaching Sofia, as the caravan which he had accompanied thus far broke up here, while his own Janissary, having in him, as he says, "more of the Merchant than the Souldier," stubbornly refused to go any further for fear of being pressed into the war.

He reluctantly took his leave of the friendly *spahis* who had proved so good-natured towards a chance-met *ghiaur*, and heading southwards continued his journey towards Constantinople. The remainder of his travels and his long disquisitions on Turkish customs and morals, though abounding in interest, would be out of place in this chapter and it is time to introduce the other "adventurer" whose acquaintance with the fighting Turk, though as intimate as Blunt's, was made from a very different standpoint.

CHAPTER IX

TWO MARTIAL ADVENTURES

(2)

Our anonymous diarist was a volunteer enrolled in the army of the famous Polish general Chodkiewiez. In the year 1622 this army was sent by Sigismund III to oppose the advance of Sultan Osman II who was marching with a host of Turks against Podolia, accompanied by his ally the Krim of Tartary and the usual horde of Tartar auxiliaries.

The Christians, who on their side were assisted by large numbers of Russian cossacks from the Don and the Volga, had marched down to the borders of Bessarabia and crossing the Dniester at no great distance from Kamenets had entrenched themselves round the little town of Chocin lying in a bend on the southern bank of the river. The Turks, marching northward, had crossed the Pruth at the end of August and contact was established between the two armies on September 2nd on which day, to quote the first entry in the diary, "the Turkes and Tartars encamped themselves by us within a mile or halfe a mile." The Christian force held a bridge-head, apparently of a mile or two radius, with wooded country separating their own from the Turkish lines. These the enemy, true to their old proud traditions, had left unentrenched, "scorning" as the writer says, "to quarter themselves within Ditches." The auxiliaries of each army guarded its flanks, while the Tartars as usual scoured and pillaged all the surrounding country.

Such was the position of the two forces when fighting began. A reconnaissance by the Turks on September 3rd led to no results as the Christians had orders "to remain within their tents and trenches and play among the Turkes with their greate Artillery."

An incident occured, however, in the evening which closely affected the future course of the operations. Prince Ladislas, King Sigismund's son, was marching into the camp with supplies and reinforcements when the bridge broke and left the army stranded on the further bank. The results, as will appear later, nearly brought disaster to the Polish force.

On the 4th September the Cossacks repulsed a Turkish attack, making "so brave a salley, that they put the Turkes to flight even to their tents, with such a slaughter, and such a successe, that they surprised their Artillery, tooke many Tents, and carried with them much furniture, and so returned before dark night with the booty, to their own Camp and lodging."

Three days later the Turks made a more serious attempt to break through the lines which is described as follows : "The seaventh of September the Turkes came upon us againe in the after noone, and very outragiously in great companies assaulted our Bulwarkes, which were yet unperfected, and lay somewhat naked to opposition, ascending the same, and taking as it were possession: but with equall losse, as it appeared for the time, untill the noble Lord Steward of the Kingdome, who came there by chance with his troope of Horse, set upon them most valiantly, and put them off the walls

to a fore-flight, as farre as the wood scited even before
the Turkes Campe, whither they followed them in the
slaughter. The assault endured from noone to night
and with so fearfull effects that the multitude of the
slaughtered lay in heapes in the fields. Yea, it was
remarkable, how all that night the Turkes made a search
with lighted fire-brands, and other Lamps, for some
person of account amongst the dead bodies, which as
some of their owne fugitives affirmed, was one of the
Viceer Baffas, who, was missing, and could not be
found."

Rain interfered on the following day and although
"both Armies drawne up in battaile array stood looking
upon one another even to Sunne setting," no more
fighting actually took place beyond a little affray with
the Tartar horsemen who "inconsiderately came upon
the Cossacks againe."

The Turks meanwhile took advantage of the col-
lapse of the bridge, which the Poles were making frantic
efforts to rebuild, to occupy a position in their rear and
transported their guns across the river to a point where
they could play upon the Cossacks' quarters and interfere
with the repairing of the bridge. A brilliant sortie,
however, drove them out of their new positions, for
which our hero was duly grateful. "God graunt" says
he "wee may be thankfull for these things. For without controversie, Gods onely hand hath protected us,
that both on the one side the Turke is more remiss
than his former threatnings, and this present appearance
promised; and we on the other side, we have had
greater courages, and better successe than wee could
any manner of way expect."

Every success of the Christian arms is in the same

way devoutly ascribed to the help of the Almighty.
On September 15th, for example, the enemy made
another determined attack "neither fearing our Artillery,
nor making accompt of our Trenches: the great Turke
himselfe being a spectator on an eminent Hill, whose
youth apprehended the mischiefe but as a sport. For
without any manner of remorce for the perishing of so
many thousands, they came forward like furious beasts
without Discipline or order, and so perished like beasts,
when the Artillery played upon them, and wee rushed
out as violently, well armed and appointed, in the smoake
against them. This Battaile lasted from Noone to Night,
and the God of Battailes for his mercy sake did frustrate
and annihilate both the purpose and the rage and fury
of our Enemies; nor ended it so, but for his Glories
sake wee prevailed with a great slaughter, and little
losse on our side: So that it should seeme all their
threatnings and fury was in vaine, concerning the
attempting of our Trenches, and the Angels of the Lord
spred his wings over our Tents."

By this time the situation of the Christian forces,
cut off as they were from all supplies, had grown desperate and on the 17th the Great Lord General held a
" Martiall Counsell with the Lord Senators, Dukes,
Governors and Captaines, together with the General of
the Cossacks with all his Colonels and Officers" and put
the position before them, explaining that unless provisions could be brought into the Camp within a few
days they would be faced with starvation. His doughty
officers after hearing what their leader had to say "with
one voyce and unanimity of Spirit concluded and agreed
rather to die manfully in the field than to goe backe
one foot of ground or give the Enemy cause of pre-

sumption." This spirited resolution was followed by
prompt action. A nobleman named Koskakorffski
volunteered to make an expedition to Kamenets and
try to smuggle in stores from there. He left the camp
with a small escort but not without exciting the attention
of the Turks who, being thus forewarned, prepared to
fall on the convoy on their way back, "advancing a
strong Battalion with many shot on foote, and divers
field Pieces to intercept his returne, and so lay betweene
the Towne and our Campe, being not 15 myle assunder."

With the enemy holding the road in force there
seemed little or no hope of the convoy breaking their
way through, but in the end the feat was accomplished
by a very neat *ruse de guerre* on the part of Koskakorffski. Let me quote the incident in full.

"When the towne sawe the fields thus overspred
with Tartars so well appointed to intercept the Carriages,
considering nevertheless the necessity of relieving the
Campe, the Lord Koskakorffski with the other Captaines, thought it best to put a trick upon their Enemies,
and deceive them if they could by a petty Stratagem,
which they thus effected: When all thinges were ready
for their returne within Eight dayes after their departure
from the Campe, they set forward backe againe with
many Waggons of Wine and Corne, and so issued out
with certaine Troopes well appointed, whom they flancked
with light Waggons full of Strawe and Hay, yet not so
full but they went in a manner as fast as the Horse.
Which when the Tartars perceived, they brought up
their Pieces and came forward with their shot, to dis-
rancke these Cartes, verily supposing the maine booty
was in the midst of the troopes: but the Cartes went so
fast, and the Horse upon the trot, that they were quickly

out of shot of their Ordinance, and made the Tartars weary to follow them. Yet as they were instructed they made divers stands, as if the Waggons ment to take some rest, and then as the Tartars approached they would trot away againe, and thus they continued till night: by which time the Tartars were quickly drawne from the Towne, and thought it worke enough to secure the field Pieces from surprizing: When night came, then issued out the Lord Koskakorffski with the mayne Convoy indeed, which consisted of Corne, Oyle, Wine, Honey, and Cattle, and went a cleane contrary way unknowne to the Enemy, though somewhat about, to a Towne called Sarno Kovonicie, where he was accomodated to the River of Ister [*i.e.* Dniester]. But by that time the Turkes knew how they were deceived and, exasperated with very rage, ranne downe in whole Companies to beset the River on both sides, and brought their Ordinance to play upon the Boates, who kept the streame, but the most were passed by ere they came ; and the rest kept the Channell, which was heere so broad, that the Ordinance played on the Banckes and could not doe them much harme : Yet did the Turkes follow them as farre as our Trenches, but we having certaine Towers well fortefied on both sides the River, played out of them so violently, that wee cut off some of them in their speediness, and those who were within reach of the shot of our Trenches, were faine to recoyle, and so the Turkes and Tartars returned with great sorrow on all sides to be thus disappointed, and we entertained our friends with joy on every side to be thus releeved."

Although the Christian army was in the position of a beleaguered garrison, they were not content to remain wholly on the defensive but from time to time ventured

on night attacks which, from the detailed descriptions
given of them, bore a singular resemblance to the
organised trench raids which were a marked feature
of the fighting on the western front during the Great
War. Here is the account of one such attack.

"The 18th of September certaine Companies of
Foot made a salley out of the Cossacks quarter in the
night upon the Turkes Army, which was done so
secretly and suddenly, that they overturned many
Tents, ransacked divers Cabins, and killed some hundreds of men with Javelings, Pollaxes, and Launces,
without the report of a Peece, or carrying any Artillery
with them: yea, herein they were so fortunate, that they
returned with great spoil, without the losse of a man.
The next night they performed as much, and with the
like stratagem set upon the Bridge they had newly
builded and erected, and slew Corkan Baffaw, to whose
custody and charge it was committeed. They also killed
many Turkes, tooke nine prisoners, and returned with
great spoils and a rich prey, wherein were divers garments furred with costly Furres." It is noteworthy that
it was the enterprising Cossacks who were responsible
for these bold ventures.

Escaped prisoners from the Turkish camp were
continually creeping through the lines with news of the
enemy's preparations, and through them the Poles received warning of the Sultan's determination to throw
his whole force into a desperate and decisive assault on
one of the last days of the month.

While waiting nervously for the promised attack,
the Christian army suffered a heavy blow in the loss of
their brave General who on the 24th "after labouring
long in his sickness, and being wearied and spent againe

with intollerable convulsions and distemperature of the ayre, yeelded to the commaund of a higher Generall, and so died in the Camp." The Quarter-Master General, as the next Senior Officer, took over the command.

The Turks' "big push" was duly launched on the 27th when, says our hero, "the Emperour of Turks made a great preparation to set upon us on all sides, drawing out from their severall Quarters, both Horse, Foot, and Artillery, to oppresse and expugne us with an unresistable power and because he would make, as it were, sure worke of the matter, he acquainted *Tartar Chocin*, and he, either of necessity obeying or out of custome consenting, by breake of day brought all his Tartars to the place appointed for the expugnation. Having strongly mounted divers great Peeces and placed their gabbions about them, the Turkes played fearfully over our heads into our Camp. Then they transported over the river thirty more great Ordnance which beat continually upon ours, the Lissavonians, and the Cossacks Tents, and that for the space of divers hours, sending likewise fiery Speares, burning Darts, and sulphury Balls amongst us.

"After this, with strange assaults and fearfull violence, they pressed upon the two special passages of our Camp : in a word, wee were all in Armes, and the Cannons played on both sides as farre as they could for hurting those in their owne Quarters. At last on a suddaine with accustomed cry the Tartars gave on, and were ready to scale the trenches and enter in at the Ports. Then followed the Janizaries, as their seconds, and lastly, the Spahies and Chawses on Horseback, who by their bravery made themselves sure of the entrance, for the truth is we gave ground, and lost many men : For they pressed so thick upon us, that our shot did no good, and wee came to handey blowes within our owne trenches, till certaine Cossacks on that quarter, and Masters of Pole on ours, finding the Tartars disordered and disarmed, rushed upon them with fury that they were driven as fast back againe as they came in and they also bare down the Janizaries and pushed them much with their violence.

"Yet the Turkes still sent fresh men forward who with a strange pertinacity and unchangeable valour continued until Sun-set in the expugnation and nigh made a shrewd adventure and opened a gap of entrance into our country."

The Tartars meanwhile had found a congenial *rôle* in the battle by crossing the Dniester and making a sudden descent upon the Polish army's baggage lines from the rear. "They thought," the writer explains, "that we had left the backside of our Campe naked and undefended, but when they came, they found the Carts, Waggons, and Carriages, so strongly to Barricade it, that they thought it in vaine to hazard themselves, and so returned disappointed : yet because they would be doing, they threw wild-fire amongst the carriages, and put the cattle in a great feare, whose roarings and bel-lowings amazed us much, and in a manner begged reliefe at our hands, so that we thought it meete to send out certain Troopes of Horse, who fell upon them so oppor-tunely, that they let in 200 Polaxes amongst them, yea the very Pyoners came with their Pixes and hutches, and played their parts like men and Souldiers: So that in the end wee compelled them to swim over the River backe againe."

Throughout the whole day the Turks continued the struggle but without success for, as the diary modestly puts it, "God bethanked, with our accustomed constancy we kept our ground, and though with some losse constrayned them to let goe the hold they had, and in the end with a great shame and a greater slaughter, they hid their heades within their owne hedges."

Thus the attack was foiled and Poland saved from the Turkish irruption.   The relief which their victory brought to the heroic defenders finds words in a quaint outburst with which the diarist's account of the great battle closes.

He reviews the terrible consequences which must have ensued if the enemy had broken through.   "God knows," he says, "whither this inundation would have runne.   For you see, when raging Seas beate upon the bankes of low ground, if they prevaile in bearing them before them, whole Countries are swallowed up in the Vast paunch of the Ocean : But the same God, that puts a hooke in the nostrils of Leviathan, and bindeth Behemoth with a chayne, set a limitation for these raging Mahumetans and furious and barbarous Tartarians, over which they should not passe at this time."

Sultan Osman was furious at his defeat and for some days sulked in his Camp where, according to the reports of Christian Prisoners who subsequently returned thence, he was "so franticke that he would excruciate and torment himselfe with actions of distemperature, as throwing of his Turbane, beating his breast, and kicking his very Basshawes, who durst not reply, but were subject to a very sauish prostitution."   His thoughts turned to peace however and, not daring to risk the displeasure of the Janizaries by openly beginning negotiations, he privily conveyed to the Christian Commander that if he would send plenipotentiaries to the Turkish Camp they would find the Turks ready to settle terms. So after holding a Council of War the General elected two Commissioners "to tractate with the Turkes" and sent them accompanied by "20 of the best Gentlemen of the Campe well furnished with a flag of truce." Their reception was as follows.

"By this time the Trumpers had given warning of their accesse, and when they approached very neere the Turkes Camp 200 Spahies and Chawses on Horsebacke with Velvet Gownes, rich silver Maces, and brave Turbanes, came to entertaine them, and bring them by way of conduction through the first Guard of Janizaries, and so through many Troopes of Horse, and field Pieces mounted on delicate Carriages, till they came to the Tent of the Viceer, who welcomed him in his Masters behalfe: but according to former custome hee must attend a while, ere hee could have Answer from the Grand Signeur himselfe, and peradventure not speak with him at all: For you must know, that however they were glad of composition, yet the Turke would not discover any inclination to Peace, but if he did condiscend, it was meerly out of Heroyick compassion, not any necessity of his part."

Six days were spent in discussing terms, but on October 9th peace was signed on the basis of the earlier treaty which the ambitious young Sultan had upset when he led his army against the Poles, and the Turkes withdrew again over the river Pruth.

The settlement was sealed by the usual exchange of gifts between the principals, King Sigismund sending "dogs and certaine payres of guns made in the Low-Countries," while the Sultan "regratulated" with a present of a living elephant.

CHAPTER X

A PERSIAN INTERLUDE

A collection of Italian "viaggi" published at Venice in 1543 contains the story told by himself of the "Magnifico Messer Josophat Barbaro's" mission to Uzun Hassan, the King of Persia. As the narrative bears only indirectly on Turkey some excuse is needed, perhaps, for its inclusion in the present volume. I can only plead that the book which contains it happens to be among the Turkish collection mentioned in my preface and that it gives an undoubtedly interesting glimpse of Turkey's great Mohammedan neighbour.

"The long Hassan" (to render his name into English) was indeed closely related to the Turks as leader of the "White Sheep," a Turcoman horde centred round Diar Bekir. By dint of fighting he had made himself 'King' of Persia—at that time barely emerging from the wreckage of Tamerlane's empire—though he had a rival who challenged his title from the distant capital of Herat. A bond of union had arisen between Venice and this Turcoman chief in their common enmity to the Turks who were busily engaged in chasing the Venetians out of the archipelago while at the same time expanding their empire eastward at Persia's expense.

With the object of arranging for a concerted plan of action against Turkey, the Signoria of Venice deputed Messer Barbaro to travel to Tabriz and discuss things with Hassan. He left Venice accordingly in 1471 and sailed to Cyprus, the first stage of his journey, with a strong naval escort. There he landed and exchanged civilities with King James, the last of the dynasty established on the throne of Cyprus by our own King Richard at the time of the third crusade. Incidentally he lent a hand in the intrigue then forward for annexing the island to Venice while at the same time making arrangements for his long overland journey through Asia Minor.

Luckily for him the Ottomans had not yet consolidated the whole of the Anatolian provinces, and the Sultan of Caramania, whose coast faces on to Cyprus, was at that particular moment at war with Mohammed the Conqueror. Barbaro first of all aided the Sultan by landing a force of marines and reducing a couple of forts held by Ottoman garrisons, then disembarked his own party near Mersina and started on his perilous journey.

His way lay through Adana, Urfa and Mardin to Sirt on the Tigris. We need not stay to accompany him on his route except to mention his naïve belief that Mardin, perched on the top of its towering cliff, was of such an altitude that no bird could fly over it, and his delight in Sirt—which must in his day have been a remarkably flourishing town—with its beautiful mosques and fountains and bridge over the Tigris so high above the stream that, to use his own phrase, a full rigged ship with all sail set could easily have passed under it.

On entering Kurdistan Barbaro was struck by the murderous appearance of the Kurds. He was soon to make an intimate acquaintance with these inveterate brigands.

9—2

The caravan was crossing the great mountain range between Van and Urmia[1] when it was attacked by a party of them who killed Barbaro's *cancelliero*, as well as the Persian ambassador returning home from Venice in Barbaro's company, and stole all the baggage. Barbaro himself was slightly wounded while escaping on horseback up the mountain side; he succeeded, however, in getting clear away and, falling in presently with a band of pilgrims, accompanied them, by way of Khoy, safely to Tabriz.

Barbaro had left Venice well loaded with presents from the Signoria for Uzun Hassan—gold and silver plate, silks and woollens and rolls of the famous scarlet cloth which was a "spécialité" of his native town. All these, with his personal belongings, had remained in the hands of the Kurds and he arrived at Hassan's residence utterly destitute, with nothing but the clothes he stood in and not even a hat. He sent a messenger at once to Uzun Hassan to acquaint him with his misadventures and the present sorry plight in which he found himself. The Shah sent his condolences with a promise to make good his losses, a couple of suits of silk, a piece of cotton for a turban (one wonders what sort of a job the old Venetian made of it) and a sum of twenty ducats.

Being thus restored to self-respect, Barbaro went to pay his respects to Hassan and present the letters he had brought with him from Venice.

His description of Hassan's court gives an impression of barbaric luxury touched with the whimsical

---

[1] By a rather curious coincidence this is precisely the place where the author of the present book was similarly attacked and wounded by Kurdish tribesmen in the autumn of 1914.

delicacy which is characteristic of all things Persian. The Shah lived in a kind of garden palace which, though beautifully appointed, did not at all reflect the stolid splendours of the Ottoman court. On going to his audience Barbaro was led into a walled quadrangle, carefully turfed, with a sand path leading up to a *loggia* in the centre of one side. A fountain and basin occupied the middle of the *loggia* and by the side of the basin Hassan sat on a gold embroidered cushion with his scimitar and a water-jug ready to hand, sheltered from the sun by an overhanging canopy supported from the branches of trees. The floor was strewn with beautiful carpets and the walls covered with painted tiles. A company of singers and musicians playing on harps, lutes, and cymbals, discoursed music at the further end of the *loggia*.

After settling affairs of state, Hassan courteously invited the Venetian envoy to a tournament to be held on the following day on the great *maidan*. Barbaro accepted and betook himself next day to the place, where he found a crowd of four or five thousand on-lookers, half of them mounted like himself on horse-back. A number of different sort of games and displays took place, but the great feature of the day was a wolf-fight. The wolves were led on by cords tied to their hind-legs and loosed one by one against the wolf-fighter. The latter was armed with a knife and had his left forearm swathed in a sash. With his padded limb he warded off the wolf's attacks till he found a chance of driving his knife into the creature's heart. Incidentally the savage rushes of the maddened beasts so terrified the spectators' horses, that, as Barbaro recounts, they broke and fled in every direction, falling over each other and plunging many of their riders into a canal bordering the *maidan*. A similar sort of entertainment, he mentions, took place every Thursday for the Shah's diversion.

Shortly after Barbaro's arrival an embassy reached Tabriz from one of the Indian princes, who, as a descendant of Tamerlane, was related to the Persian ruler. The envoys brought magnificent presents consisting largely of wild animals and they paraded these in front of Hassan and his officers, Barbaro also being present. The beasts were led past by keepers, the more dangerous of them being secured by chains. There were a lion and lioness, a very fierce leopardess, two civet cats, a giraffe ("animal bellissimo" Barbaro calls it, and proceeds to describe it as a long-necked creature, short haired like an ass, with horns like a goat, a head like a stag,· but "più polita" and a tongue the length of one's arm), cages of parrots and cockatoos, and lastly a couple of elephants who performed tricks such as levelling trees by leaning against them.

Afterwards the chief envoys sat down with the Shah in the *loggia* and had the inanimate presents brought in by their servants. A string of a hundred slaves came with bales of cotton, six men with fine silks thrown over their arms, nine with silver cups full of rare stones, others with porcelain basins and ewers, aloes and sandal wood and finally a number of men carrying poles with packets of specie slung from them.

After the ceremony the Shah sent for Barbaro to come to his private room, a delightful little chamber with walls panelled in silk and a beautiful door of sandal wood inlaid with gold wire and pearls. Here he exhibited his treasures, rubies from India, pearls from the

Persian Gulf, vases from China and antique cameos, probably recovered from Hellenic or Sassanian ruins. One of these last was engraved with the head of a Greek goddess and Barbaro was much entertained when the Shah, in showing it him, asked if it were not a portrait of the Blessed Virgin Mary!

About this time one of Hassan's sons raised the standard of revolt at Shiraz and his father marched south to quell the rebellion. Barbaro went also and describes the march, or rather one should say the migration, for the Shah and his Turcomans, following their nomadic instincts, took most of their property, including their families, with them. The endless caravan, half-a-day's journey from first to last, meandered across Persia, the men and women on horseback and the babies in paniers. Barbaro enumerates the animals which composed the train; 20,000 riding horses, many covered with armour, 5000 horses of burden, an equal number of pack-mules, 2000 donkeys and 30,000 camels. The actual fighting force consisted of 15,000 swordsmen, 1000 archers, and 8000 common soldiers on foot, with a host of armourers, cobblers, tailors and other supernumeraries. The children of under ten alone numbered 6000. For sporting purposes there were 100 hunting leopards, 3000 greyhounds (Persia is the home of the breed) and 200 falcons "gentili e villani." Two thousand led-horses beautifully caparisoned belonging to the various chieftains, accompanied the army, and to crown all there were no fewer than eight thousand two-humped dromedaries adorned with bells and trappings embroidered in gold with Koranic texts, which carried no loads and were for pure ostentation. The Shah with a personal guard of 500 horsemen was preceded by numbers of runners continually shouting to clear the road.

They marched down through Kum, famous then as now for its blue-glazed earthenware, Ispahan, a mere mound of ruins ever since Tamerlane had, a hundred years before, razed it level with the ground and massacred every living soul within it, and Yezd (at that time the great emporium where merchants met from Turkey, Tartary and Hindustan), till the rebel prince was finally met and subdued on the borders of Fars. Then the great host returned again in the same manner to its starting place.   On the march the traditions of his cruel predecessor were worthily upheld by the Shah, who on one occasion, learning that a certain old chieftain was intriguing with his son, had him brought before him trussed and skewered like a partridge!

Barbaro had one more experience after returning to Tabriz which is worth recording.   It was a sort of *fête champêtre* to celebrate the circumcision of two of Hassan's sons.   A large number of tents were set up for the merry-makers in a field of young corn.   First there were wrestling bouts, which must have been of a peculiarly brutal nature as Barbaro mentions that the champion was excused from wrestling because he had killed several of his opponents on the last occasion. Then there were foot-races and, lastly, races for the professional "runners" who, naked except for a leather apron and oiled all over "to preserve their energies," trotted incredible distances, some of the Shah's own runners being actually credited with ten days on end without a stop.

The prizes were heaped in one of the tents and consisted chiefly of silk dresses and saddles.   Some had a touch of the grotesque, as, for instance, an enormous sugar-loaf hat covered with *pompons*, which stood on the ground in front of the tent. When the time came the Shah sent a servant to clap it on the head of the winner who was then commanded to dance in it before the assembled company. Barbaro himself, with other distinguished guests, was presented in the course of the proceedings with an enormous iced cake brought in by two men on a large wooden tray and surrounded with little cups of fruit and coloured sweets. He does not tell us how he disposed of such a "white elephant."

Shortly after these festivities there arrived at Tabriz another embassy which had travelled from Venice by the very arduous and circuitous route through Austria and Russia, and Messer Josophat Barbaro returned home to his native city to render an account of his mission and describe to the wondering Venetians the marvels of Uzun Hassan's Court.

CHAPTER XI

THE SULTAN'S NAVY

There is a story which used to be current among "Frankish" circles at Pera of a Turkish High Admiral who was sent, much against his nature, on a cruise to Malta and, on returning some months later, was summoned to give a report to the Sultan. "Well," said the Monarch, "what sort of a place is Malta?" The admiral's answer was terse and conclusive; all he said was "*Malta yok*" which, freely rendered, means "there ain't no Malta." He had searched for it in vain all round the Mediterranean!

The story owed much of its zest to the sight familiar to dwellers in Constantinople of the Turkish fleet perennially anchored in the Golden Horn, and I quote it here merely as a parable of Turkish inaptitude for navigation. Yet in Suleyman's day the Turkish navy swept the ocean and on one occasion at least put to rout the combined navies of the great Mediterranean Powers. The paradox is easily explainable; the Turkish navy of the old days was hardly Turkish at all; half of it was corsair and the remaining half recruited almost entirely from among Christians, renegades and prisoners. The horrible life of the Christian galley-slaves is described in the concluding chapters of this book. They shared their miserable existence with convicts from the jails and ordinary slaves hired out by their lawful

owners for the summer months—the only part of the
year in which the fleet was ordinarily mobilized—at so
many *aspers* the season. One may note in passing
a curious consequence of this method of recruitment,
which was that on board Turkish men-of-war objects
were named, and orders were given, not in Turkish but
in the bastard Italian which serves to the present day
as the *lingua franca* of the Levant[1]. Only the militia
carried in the larger ships was genuinely Turkish, being
raised mainly by the same system as prevailed in the
army, a certain proportion of *zaïms* and timariots holding
their lands as sea-fiefs and being pledged to render
service, either in person or by proxy, at sea instead of
on land.

The best of the ships themselves, especially in the
seventeenth century, were prizes captured from the
Christians. Blunt, influenced perhaps by national pre-
judice, declares that in his time the majority of them
were Dutch, because, he asserts, the Dutchmen, who
did a large carrying trade in the Mediterranean, lacked
the pluck to fight and when attacked took advantage
of the Turkish custom of liberating the crews of ships
which struck their colours without firing a shot. English
ships, he adds, besides being better armed, were less
sought after by the Turks because they were slow goers
and consequently of less use as men-of-war. He took
care, however, to disabuse the Turks of any miscon-
ceptions they might form of England's naval power, and
when asked how his country could claim the mastery of
the seas when possessing such slow craft, answered
"that these ships which came into their [the Turks']

---

[1] By a curious contradiction we, on our side, derive the term "admiral"
from the Turkish corsairs, corrupting it from the arabic *Amir-ul-bahr*.

Seas were private merchantmen, slugs only made for
burthen and weather: but for Warre our King had
a Navy Royall of another frame, the best for sail and
fight in the World."

An amusing sketch which he gives elsewhere of
Turkish sailors on a small sailing ship in which he
travelled as passenger deserves quotation for its own
sake. " I," he says, "who had often proved the Bar-
barisme of other nations at sea, and above all of our
owne, supposed myself among Beares, untill by experience I found the contrarie, and that, not only in ordinary
civilitie but with so ready service, such a patience and
so sweet and gentle a way as made me doubt if it was
a dreame or reall. If at any time I stood in their way
or encombered their ropes, they would call me 'janum[1],'
a term of great affection among them and that with an
incline, a voice and a gesture so respectful as assured
me their other words (which I understood not) were of
the same strain.

" Nor were they irreligious; thus all the Voyage
morning and evening they would salute the Sunne with
three great shouts and a priest saying a kind of Litanie,
every prayer ending with 'Macree Kirchoon' (*sic*) that
is 'be Angels present' and the people answered 'Amen,
Amen.'"

In the same way that the Turks depended on their
Tartar auxiliaries in land warfare, they leaned—but in
a far greater degree—on their corsair allies at sea.
The link between them was naturally a loose one, for
the Barbary corsairs, even when nominally under the
Sultan's dominion, could act pretty well as they liked

---

[1] i.e. "my soul," commonly used between Turks in the same sense as
we say "old fellow."

A WARSHIP PASSING BETWEEN THE CASTLES OF EUROPE AND OF ASIA

From George Sandys' *Travels*, 1632

with but little fear of retribution. They appreciated, however, the value of Ottoman prestige and both parties gained by uniting their forces against the Christian world. The haughty Turk looked, indeed, somewhat askance at his ally as a professional pirate, but he was glad enough of his help against the Venetian or Spaniard and by no means disdained a share in casual plunder. The Turks owed a great deal also to the fourteen Beys of the Archipelago who contributed a galley a-piece to the Sultan's fleet whenever it put to sea; in the summer season when they joined the navy the prizes they took were claimed by the Sultan, but the Beys were free to pirate what they could on their own account in the winter months.

The mention of the corsairs brings us to that romantic figure, the greatest of Turkish sea captains, Khaireddin Barbarossa. Barbarossa's life is so much an epitome of Turkey's sea power that, even at the risk of repeating facts already well known to the reader, I will include a short sketch of his career. His autobiography, written in his old age at the command of his master, Suleyman II, has been handed down in a paraphrased form in the pages of Hajji Khalifa, a Turkish naval historian of the early seventeenth century (whose work was translated into English about a hundred years ago by James Mitchell), so we are fortunate in being able to go to the fountain head for our knowledge.

Khizr Khaireddin and his brothers, Oruj, Ishak and Elias were the sons of a peasant of Mitylene of Christian descent, and like most of the Archipelago islanders, took to the sea at an early age. In other words they were born pirates. In an encounter with a Rhodian galley (the island was at the time still in the possession of the Knights) one of the brothers, Elias, lost his life and the others were taken prisoners and were for some time slaves in Rhodes. Ishak from this point vanishes from the scene but Khizr and Oruj, having escaped from Rhodes and obtained from Sultan Bayezid the Turkish equivalent of letters of marque, set up in partnership as privateers. They had spent a few profitable years in this occupation, ranging the Aegean by summer and wintering snugly at Alexandria, when the new Sultan, Selim, issued a decree against free-lancing pirates, and the brothers were driven to offer their services to Sultan Hassan of Tunis, the last of the independent dynasty of the Beni Hafs. They were given by him a stronghold on the coast and a free hand to plunder Christian shipping on condition of surrendering half the proceeds to the Sultan. Those were the golden days of Barbary piracy and the brothers soon amassed a respectable fortune, sometimes taking as many as 20 ships and 3000 prisoners in a single month. The prisoners—ravaged for the most part from small fishing villages on the Italian coast—they sold wholesale in the Tunisian slave markets at a florin ahead.

Their ambition grew with their success and they presently transferred themselves to Algiers where Khizr proclaimed himself as an independent sultan. The establishment of such a hornet's nest on the opposite coast seriously alarmed the Spaniards who sent a fleet to annihilate the upstart sultan. The fleet and not the sultan, suffered annihilation, the engagement, according to Hajji Khalifa's account, resulting as follows:

" The Admiral Ferdinand from Spain entered the harbour with a fleet of one hundred and ten ships. Khair-ad-din immediately came into the harbour and after a hot engagement entirely routed the infidels. The Admiral's ship struck on the sand, when, in despair, he and six hundred infidels jumped overboard, and with thirty-six captains, and in all about three thousand men, were made prisoners. Two prisons underground were filled with them, and the city was crowded with those assigned to the natives. Some of them formed a conspiracy, and had made arrangements for their escape but were detected. Soon after a messenger arrived from Spain offering 100,000 ducats for the ransome of the thirty-six officers. To this the Ulemas would not give their consent, saying that the captains being expert in naval matters, and everyone of them brave fellows, the sum ought to be doubled: this, however, was not effected. Khair-ad-din then sought some pretence for having them killed; and when he heard of their attempt to escape, ordered a general execution. For the body of the Admiral Ferdinand seven thousand florins were offered; but the Moslem considering it improper to deal in carcases, threw it into a deep well."

It was soon after this event that the first encounter took place between Barbarossa and his life-long enemy Andrea Doria.

The appearance on the scene of the great Genoese patriot is described with characteristic bombast by the Turkish historian. "When the infidel could no longer navigate the sea," he says, "and there was no safety along their coasts, the King of Spain called a council to determine what measures to adopt against Barbarossa. Andrea Doria, one of the most valiant admirals of Spain taking his hat in his hand said, if the king of France would give him twenty of his galleys, he would venture to attack Barbarossa." The French ships were supplied and Doria was about to set out for Algiers when Khair-eddin forestalled the attack by sailing with his corsair fleet into the Gulf of Lyons. He laid an ambush off Marseilles but his plans were defeated by the brave captain of a vessel, captured by the corsairs on its way to Majorca with a cargo of cheeses, who escaped and gave information to the Christian Commander-in-chief. Doria, however, feeling too weak to fight Barbarossa until he had received a reinforcement of several galleys from his native town which were on their way to join him, slipped by the corsairs and took shelter in a Spanish port. Barbarossa getting in his turn intelligence of the enemy's movements, waylaid the Genoese detachment and captured them with all their crews, including, as the record says, "twenty men of rank and captains and a hundred and twenty brave infidels who wore golden chains about their necks." A ransom of 20,000 pieces of gold was offered for the prisoners by the Genoese, but Barbarossa refused to deal and put the unlucky victims to death *en masse*.

For some time the two great seamen fought for the upper hand in the Western Mediterranean, manœuvring endlessly to cut off each other's ships and pitting their wits against each other in every manner of ruse. Doria, for instance, sent one of his officers with a barge of valuable merchandise to cruise about off Algiers with the express purpose of getting captured and giving a false report of his intention to attack the town. Which duly happened but with small gain to Doria, for Barbarossa saw through the stratagem and weaved a plot of his own, ostensibly unmanning his fleet and digging trenches as though in preparation for the attack, until the crew of the captured barge, whom he generously allowed to return home, had left with the news, when he at once mobilized his ships and slipped off to raid the Italian coast.

In the meantime Selim, who had put the embargo on Barbarossa's early Aegean exploits, died and Suleyman came to the throne. He at once showed the strength of his arm by capturing Rhodes and attacking Vienna. Barbarossa, seeing how the wind was blowing, took the great decision of his life and abandoned the freedom of a sea-rover and independent corsair-king in favour of the more secure dignity of a liege of the Ottoman Sultan. He therefore left his brother Oruj in charge of Algiers and sailed with most of his fleet and presents of fabulous value to Constantinople, where he paid homage to Suleyman. The Sultan at once made him Capudan Pasha, or Lord High Admiral, at the same time confirming him in the sultanate of Algiers under his own suzerainty. Barbarossa lost no time in taking in hand the Turkish fleet which he entirely reorganised, building numbers of new ships and adding his own Algerian vessels. With this remodelled fleet, the greatest the Turks had ever known, Barbarossa launched a series of marauding expeditions into all parts of the Mediterranean, terrorizing all Christian shipping and ravaging the coasts of Italy, France and Spain, Sardinia, the Balearic Islands and even the Adriatic coast. A more serious campaign for the capture of Corfu, undertaken with a hundred and thirty-five galleys and thirty thousand sailors and accompanied by Suleyman in person and two of his sons, failed after a determined siege, and the Venetians successfully repulsed several attempts against Crete; the Turks captured, on the other hand, a number of the Venetian islands in the Eastern Mediterranean. In

the matter of plunder the operations were highly re-
munerative, one single expedition bringing over half-a-
million pieces of gold into the exchequer besides other
booty. The admiral meanwhile enriched himself beyond
the dreams of avarice but was careful to propitiate his
royal employer by handsome gifts. "On the morning
after his arrival," says the Hajji, describing the return
of the fleet from a season's cruise, "the pasha dressed
two hundred boys in scarlet, bearing in their hands
flasks and goblets of gold and silver. Behind them
followed thirty others, each carrying on his shoulders
a purse of gold; after these came two hundred men,
each carrying a purse of money; and lastly, two hundred
infidels wearing collars, each bearing a roll of cloth on
his back. These he took as a present to the Emperor,
and having kissed the royal hand, was presented with
robes of the most splendid kind, and received the highest
marks of honour; for never at any period had any
capudan done such signal service."

On June 8th, 1538, Barbarossa sailed from the Porte
on the greatest exploit of his life, a desperate struggle
with the fleets of Spain, Portugal, Genoa, Venice and
the Papal States, united under the command of Doria.
The alliance had been formed in a determined attempt
to free the Mediterranean from the incubus of the red-
bearded pirate, and the fleets assembled for the purpose
at Corfu. Khaireddin as soon as he heard of the alliance
set out to meet the enemy. When he came near Corfu,
being uncertain of their exact position, he prayed for
divine guidance and was rewarded by a vision of a great
shoal of fish rising from the sea in the direction of the
Gulf of Arta on the Albanian coast. Setting his course
accordingly he sailed on and when near Prevesa his

look-out reported the Christian fleet in sight. Barbarossa invoked the aid of Allah, inscribed some verses
of the Koran on slips of paper which he scattered on
the waves on either side of his ship, and steered to the
attack. The action which followed is historic. The
huge Spanish galleons on which Doria chiefly relied
fared no better than those which the Duke of Sidonia
led against Drake fifty years later, and the day ended
in a complete victory for the Turk. The story of the
battle is told in the Hajji's pages as follows:

"The enemy's light vessels came up to the strait
[of Prevesa] where the arrogant wretches opened fire
upon the Moslem vessels. The brave and experienced
Pasha, unable to bear this insolence, beat his drum and
cymbals, hoisted his flags and sailed out of the bay to
meet the fleet of the despicable enemy.

"The unfortunate infidels, stationing themselves in
regular lines, now began to discharge their artillery;
which, however, wanted strength to make it efficient.
A galleon first came out and opened a heavy fire, but
was driven back by the fire of the fleet. Khair-ad-din
succeeded in taking several barges by attacking them
from a distance, and thus gradually weakening them.
Andrea Doria and the general having now come up
with their galleys, were about to commence an attack,
when the brave Pasha bore down upon them, and commenced a heavy fire, which obliged them to bring round
their barges. The balls from the barges now fell like
rain, and the two fleets were so enveloped in smoke,
that they could not see each other. The enemy's galleys
several times attempted to take the Moslem vessels in
the rear, that so they might take up a position between
them and the other ships and barges. The latter, which,

from their size resembled floating castles, were dashing
against each other with great violence ; nor was it
possible to separate them.   At length, after nine of the
barges had been driven back by the strength of the
Moslem vessels, the pasha of lion-like courage redoubled
his exertions, and keeping up a brisk fire, sunk several,
and clearing a way through them, passed on to the
galleys, strictly prohibiting his men from plundering a
single barge.   The infidels were astonished, and overwhelmed with terror at the impetus of the warriors: and
their galleys being unable any longer to maintain the
fight, they turned their faces to flight.   The slaughter
continued during the whole of the interval between the
two hours of prayer and most of the barges were either
destroyed or sunk by the cannon.   Andrea Doria seeing
this tore his beard, and took to flight, all the smaller
galleys following him."

The victory left the Turks with the definite mastery
of the Mediterranean, a mastery which they retained
until their still more famous encounter with an allied
Christian fleet at the battle of Lepanto.

Four years after the battle of Prevesa, Francis I
enlisted Suleyman as his ally against the Emperor
Charles, and Barbarossa sailed to Toulon to join the
French fleet.   The campaign was not particularly noteworthy except for this unnatural union between the
most Christian King and the Caliph of Islam.   The
strangeness of the alliance was accentuated by an incident
which befell when the two fleets were anchored side by
side at Nice.   When Sunday came the church bells rang
out across the harbour and reached Barbarossa's ears.
The hateful sound, identified with the religion of the
despised Nasarinis, infuriated the devout old pirate

who at once sent a message to say that he would brook no other summons to prayer than the Muezzin's call as long as Moslems and Moslem ships remained in harbour.

The sultan of Tunis who had given Khizr and Oruj Khaireddin their start in life had long before been defeated and deposed by the Spaniards, who for a number of years held Tunis as a Spanish possession. Barbarossa, however, had held firm in his own sultanate of Algiers, which he governed chiefly by proxy. The emperor now in 1541 made a last desperate effort to oust the corsair from his lair. Charles led a fleet in person to Algiers with 50,000 men, including 4000 cavalry, on board. The fortune which followed Barbarossa through life helped him again on this occasion. A fearful storm caught Charles's fleet just as it reached the African shore and scattered it in all directions. One hunded and six of the Spanish ships were driven on shore, fourteen hundred Moslem galley-slaves escaped to freedom and Charles returned discomfited to Spain.

Five years later Khaireddin died at the age of eighty, the date of his death being incorporated, in the favourite Turkish fashion, in a chronogram which runs "*māt raïs ul bahr*" ("dead is the lord of the seas"). The Genoese hero who had fought him in many waters outlived him by fifteen years, dying in 1561 at the yet maturer age of ninety-two.

The period of Barbarossa's exploits produced many other admirals famous for ever in Turkish history. Turgud, "the drawn sword of Islam," a Christian born and at one time in his career a slave in Doria's galleys, and Pialé, the conqueror of Tripoli, rank second only to Khaireddin himself. Their names, like his, are associated chiefly with the Mediterranean. But there were others who won their fame in more distant waters, for Turkish seamen contributed their full share of adventure in that great age of exploration. Without boasting a Columbus or Magellan, Turkey can claim many a bold spirit who, sailing unchartered seas, added his quota to the world's knowledge of geography and navigation.

The sphere of their adventures lay chiefly in the Red Sea, the Indian Ocean and the Persian Gulf, then almost unexplored except by a few of the Portuguese captains. As early as 1530 Sultan Suleyman sent his namesake Khadim Suleyman Pasha to help the King of Gujerat against the Portuguese settlers. The expedition failed in its object after a month's vain siege of the Portuguese stronghold at Div, and in the reaction following on their defeat the Turks lost Aden. Another admiral, Piri Pasha—famous for his works on the science of navigation—recovered Aden some years later and, sailing on round the coast of Arabia and taking Muscat on his way, anchored with a Turkish fleet at Basra. He found it easier, however, to get into the Persian Gulf than out again as the Portuguese held the straits of Ormuz, and on the return he lost half of his ships and his head as well when he reached the capital. For years the remnant of his fleet remained shut up in the Gulf and many attempts were made to save them. At last Saïdi Ali, a famous astronomer and poet, retrieved his country's reputation by defeating the Portuguese near Ormuz and freeing a passage for the ships. The experiences of his fleet while returning through the Arabian Sea are graphically described in Hajji Khalifa's history.

"In the neighbourhood of Zaffer," the writer says, "they were overtaken by the storm called the *Elephant*, before which they scudded, being unable even to carry the foresail: Compared with this, a storm in the Mediterranean is as insignificant as a grain of sand: day could not be distinguished from night, and the waves rose like huge mountains. Their vessels were thus greatly injured and they were obliged to throw overboard a great part of their ammunition and stores. In this way they drifted before the wind for ten days, during which time it rained incessantly and there was no appearance of daylight. The sailors here saw immense fishes, of the length of two galleys; at which their spirits rose, because they consider them animals of good omen. They also saw sea-horses, huge serpents, tortoises as large as millstones and seaweed. After having been detained a long time, they at last approached the bay of Chekd.

" Suddenly the colour of the sea became changed to a whitish hue, and the sailors began to cry out. The cause of their alarm was what in the Indian Ocean was called a whirlpool, a thing very common about Gerdefoon on the Ethiopian coast, and in the bay of Chekd near Sind. It is stated in maritime works that ships getting into one of these must inevitably perish. Having sounded and found they had only five fathoms of water, they took in their sails. Towards morning the wind fell a little and they sent up an able seaman to the mast-head, who descried a temple on the land. Soon after they passed Kormian, Mangalore, and Somnat and came very near Div ; but the latter place being in the hands of the infidels, they did not show their sail that day, but made the best of their way. Again the wind increased, and the helms became quite unmanageable; the boatswain's whistle could not be distinguished from the whistling of the wind and no one could walk the decks. They were also obliged to shut up most of the troops in the holds. In short the horrors of this day were comparable only to those of the resurrection. At length they reached the coast of Guzerat, in India, when the sailors suddenly cried out that a hurricane was before them; upon which they dropped anchor; but the sea was so heavy that the ships were nearly upset. The galley slaves broke their chains, and all the men stripping themselves naked, began to provide themselves with barrels and leather bottles for their escape. Some of the anchors however broke and thus the vessels escaped the hurricane. This occurred at a place between Div and Daman. Towards afternoon the weather became somewhat fairer, which enabled them to proceed to the port of Daman in the district of Guzerat, where they anchored about two miles from the shore. For five days the hurricane continued to blow with great violence, and was accompanied with incessant rains. The vessels had now shipped much water, and three of them, losing their anchorage drifted ashore; but all on board landed in safety."

The era of Turkey's greatness at sea was as short as it was brilliant. It had reached its climax when Pius V in 1571 formed the Maritime League to break the Ottoman supremacy in the Mediterranean. Don Juan of Austria in command of the massed fleets proved more than a match for Muezzin-zadeh Ali, at that time Capudan Pasha, and at the battle of Lepanto (in which, by the way, the author of *Don Quixote* fought and had his left hand maimed for life by a bullet), the Ottoman navy was practically wiped off the sea.

Turkey escaped, it is true, the full results of the

disaster thanks to the futile bickerings of the Christian allies and had soon built another fleet to replace that which was lost, but she never regained her former position. The race of her great admirals was extinct and her history records no more triumphs like those of Barbarossa. Venice, her old Maritime rival, drew rapidly ahead in the struggle and within a century such a change had taken place that a squadron of half-a-dozen Venetian ships could block the Dardanelles and imprison the Turks in their own waters for months on end. Delfino and the Morosinis robbed Turkey of the last vestiges of her naval prestige, the former on one occasion attacking and routing a Turkish fleet of thirty-four vessels with his own galley and three others. Sandys, writing in the first decade of the seventeenth century, says that even in his time the Egyptian tribute came overland from Cairo as the sea passage was closed to the Turks, while Rycaut half a century later disposes of Turkish sea power in the following words:

" The Turks are not likely to be Masters of this Seat of Neptune whilst they so unwillingly apply their minds to Maritime affairs and make so little use of the advantages they have for Shipping. They indeed acknowledge their inabilities in Sea-affairs and say *That God hath given the Sea to the Christians, but the Land to us.* And no doubt but that the large Possessions and Riches they enjoy on the stable Element takes off their minds from a deep attention to matters of the Sea, which is almost solely managed among them by Renegadoes who have abandoned their Faith and Country. And it is happy for Christendom that this faintness remains on the Spirits of the Turks and aversion from all Naval employment, whose number and power the

Great God of Hosts hath restrained by the bounds of the Ocean as He hath limited the Ocean itself by the Sands of the Sea-shore."

Having looked at the exploits of Turkey's great admiral through the eyes of one of his compatriots let us now turn to a similar scene described by the pen of a Christian writer. In 1560 a Christian alliance was formed for the purpose of ousting the Turks from the island of Jerba one of their main strongholds on the North African coast. Doria himself led the fleet, which counted 200 sail, with Don Alvarez de Sande, Duke of Medina, in command of the troops. Their first attack was successful and they established a garrison on the island. As soon as the news of this reached Suleyman he sent Pialé with the Turkish fleet to repel the intruders. A hard fought battle ended in the total defeat of Doria and the garrison remained stranded on the island. The brave little force withstood a siege of several months, but, decimated by famine and disease, was finally forced to capitulate in the early autumn.

Busbequius, the imperial ambassador whose diary fills some of the early pages of this book, was in residence at Constantinople when the victorious Turkish fleet returned to the Golden Horn and he describes the scene as follows:

"In the month of September the victorious Navy of the Turks returned to Constantinople, bringing the Christian Captives with their Gallies along with them. A joyful Spectacle for the Turks, but a sad one for the Christians that live among them! That night it lay at Anchor over against Byzantium, that so they might enter the Port the next Day in greater Pomp and Splendour. Solyman came down into an Apartment in his Gardens near the Sea-side, that from thence he might see the Prisoners ent'ring in. Don Alvarez de Sande was in the Stern of his Admiral's Galley and with him Don Sancho de Leyva and Don Bellinger de Requesne, one the Commander of the Sicilian Galleys, the other of the Neapolitan. The Galleys of the Christians were despoil'd of their Ornaments, Streamers etc., and hall'd in Barques (*sic*) that they might appear little and contemptible in the sight of the Turks. They who observed Solyman's Countenance at that time say that they perceived no sign of insolent Mirth therein, nor, when I saw him go to his Devotion the next Day, was his Face altered from its usual Hue, as if that Victory had not concerned him at all, so well was this cunning old man able to bear the Breath of his smiling Fortune. The Prisoners were afterwards brought into the *Seraglio*, but so miserably Hunger-starv'd that some could hardly stand on their Legs; others fell down in a Swoon from very Feebleness, others had Arms put upon them in a Jeer, in which Posture they died. The Turks insulted over them on every hand, promising to themselves the Empire of the whole World; 'for who shall now be able to stand before us (they said) since we have overcome the Spaniards?'"

The pitiful tale of the prisoners' subsequent fate as told in Busbequius's narrative has already been quoted in Chapter VII.

Though Blunt had no doubt good reason for his remarks as to the relative immunity from capture by the Turks enjoyed by the English "slugs," one has only to look in the pages of Hakluyt to see what a hazardous adventure a voyage in the Mediterranean was for an English ship in the sixteenth century, and I can find no more fitting end for this chapter than an account by a British sea-captain of a fight with Turkish galleys which ended in the capture of ship and crew.

"'*The three halfe moones*,' manned with 38 men and well fensed with munitions, set from Portsmouth, 1563. Falling neere the Streights they perceived themselves to be beset around with eight gallies of the Turkes in such wise that there was no way for them to flie or escape away, but that they must either yeeld or els be sunke. Which the owner perceiving, manfully encouraged his company, exhorting them valiantly to shew their manhood, shewing them that God was their God and requesting them not to faint in seeing such a heape of their enemies ready to devour them, putting them in mind of the old and ancient woorthiness of their countreymen who in the hardest extremities have alwayes most prevailed and gone away conquerors, yea and where it hath bene almost impossible.

" With other like encouragements, exhorting them to behave themselves manfully, they fell all on their knees making their prayers briefly unto God: who being all risen up again perceived their enemies by their signes and defiances bent to the spoyle, whereupon every man tooke him to his weapon.

" Then stood up one Grove, the master, being a comely man with his sword and target, holding them up in defiance against his enemies. So likewise stood up the Owner, the Master's mate, Boateswaine, Purser and every man well appointed. Nowe likewise sounded up the drums, trumpets and flutes which w^d have encouraged any man had he never so little heart in him.

" Then taketh him to his charge John Foxe, the gunner, in the disposing of his pieces and sent his bullets towards the Turkes, who likewise bestowed their pieces thrice as fast towards the Christians. But shortly they drew neere so that the bowsmen fell to their charge in sending forth their arrowes so thicke among the Gallies and also in doubling their shot so sore upon them that there were twice as many of the Turkes slaine as the number of the Christians. But the Turkes discharged so fast and so long that the ship was very sore stricken and bruised under water. Which the Turkes perceiving, made the more haste to come aboord the Shippe; which ere they could doe, many a Turke bought it deerly with the losse of their lives. Yet all was in vaine and boorded they were, where they found so hot a skirmish that it had bene better they had not meddled with the feast. For the Englishmen shewed themselves men in deed, in working manfully with their bills and halbardes; where the Owner, master, boateswaine and their company stoode to it so lustily that the Turkes were halfe dismaied. But the Boateswaine shewed himselfe valiant above the rest, for he fared amongst the Turkes like a wood Lion and there was none of them that either c^d or durst, stand in his face, till at the last there came a shot from the Turkes which brake his whistle asunder and smote him on the brest so that he fell downe, bidding them farewell and to be of good comfort encouraging them likewise to winne praise by death rather than to live captives in misery and shame. Which they hearing, indeed intended to have done, but the press and store of the Turkes was so great that they were not able long to endure but were so overpressed that they c^d not wield their weapons, by reason whereof they must needs be taken. Which none of them intended to have bene but rather to have died, except onely the master's mate who shrunke from the skirmish like a notable coward, esteeming neither the value of his name nor accounting the example of his fellowes or the miseries whereunto he should be put.

"But, in fine, so it was that the Turkes were victors. Then w^d it have grieved any hard heart to see those Infidels so violently entreating the Christians not having any respect of their manhood which they had tasted of. But no remorse or any thing els doth bridle their fierce dealing so that the Christians must needs to the Gallies to serve their new masters. And they were no sooner in them but their Garments were pulled over their eares and torne from their backes and they were set to the oares."

The sequel to this unhappy incident as told by John Foxe, the gunner, is of so dramatic a nature that, although it has no particular connection with the subject of this chapter, I cannot refrain from repeating the story in a few words. Fourteen years after the loss of " *The three halfe moones* " Foxe and such of his companions as had not in the meantime either died of hardship or been ransomed by their friends in England found themselves shut up for the winter in Alexandria. Most of them were languishing in the prison, which contained in all 266 Christian slaves of all nationalities, but Foxe, who had gained a reputation as a barber, and half-a-dozen others were allowed to ply their trades outside the prison walls. Foxe had never given up the hope of escape and, finding at last a willing confederate in the person of a Spaniard, captured 30 years before and now the privileged keeper of a "victualling house," evolved a plot for rescuing himself and the whole body of prisoners. With his friend's help he secured a number of files which he smuggled into the jail and distributed to the prisoners warning them to be ready for escape on a certain night. When the time came he repaired to the Spaniard's tavern with the other ticket-of-leave men accompanied by their Turkish guard. The Spaniard, acting on a pre-arranged plan, enveigled the guard away while the others sacked the premises for whatever instruments they could turn to use as weapons. Foxe himself "tooke to him an olde rustie sword blade without either hilt or pomell, which he made to serve his turne by bending the hand-ende instead of a pomell," while the others armed themselves "with such spits and glaives as they found in the house."

Shortly after the guard returned and as soon as he entered the house realized the situation ; whereupon turning to our hero he said—presumably in the vernacular—" O Foxe, what have I deserved of thee that thou shouldst seeke my deathe?" "Thou vilain," Foxe replied, " thou hast been a bloodsucker of many a Christian's blood, and now shaltst know what thou hast deserved." "Wherewith," the tale continues, " he lift up his bright shining sword of tenne yeares rust and stroke him so maine a blow as that his head clave asunder and he fell starke dead to the ground."

The guard having been thus satisfactorily disposed of, the plotters started for the prison and having dispatched six of the warders whom they found in the jailor's lodge, secured the keys and exchanging their improvised weapons for proper knives and swords, broke into the prison where they found the prisoners free of their shackles thanks to the imported files. Hastily barricading the landward gates (the prison stood on the harbour edge), they slipped out by a watergate and took possession of a fast Turkish galley lying just outside.

By this time the whole town was in an uproar, and the Turks, rushing to the forts which commanded the harbour's entrance, trained their guns on the galley as she headed for the sea.

" Now is the gally on flote : now have the Castles full power upon it : now is there no remedy but to sinke. The canons let flie from both sides. What man can devise to save it ? There is no man but would thinke it must needes be sunke. Yet there was not one that feared the shotte which went thundring about their eares, not yet were once scarred nor touched with five and forty shot which came from the castles. Here did God hold foorth his buckler and shieldeth the gally, for they saile away, being not once touched with the glaunce of a shot and are quickly out of the Turke's reach."

It is comforting to know that when Foxe, after this wonderful exploit, returned safely to his native land he was invited to tell his story to the Council, " who considering of the state of this man in that hee had spent and lost a great part of his youth in thraldome and bondage, extended to him their liberalitie to helpe and maintaine him in age to their right honour and to the encouragement of all true hearted Christians."

CHAPTER XII

A DRAGOMAN'S DIARY

The chapter entitled "An Audience" has already introduced the reader to Dr Antonio Benetti, dragoman[1] to the Venetian Embassy at Constantinople.

The three years which Dr Antonio spent on his mission to the Turkish capital were particularly stirring ones coinciding as they did with the second siege of Vienna, and the story of the immense preparations for the campaign and its disastrous sequel fills a great part of his diary[2], interwoven with a wealth of humbler incident. He begins with the appointment of the new ambassador to the Porte in the year 1680. With the exception of Genoa, Venice was the first European State to maintain a regular embassy at Constantinople and on account of her leading position in the Levant trade there was always a vast amount of diplomatic business to be settled between the two Governments. The selection of a new *bailo* was therefore an important affair of state, especially on this occasion when full diplomatic relations were to be resumed for the first time since peace had been declared after the twenty years' war ending in the Turkish conquest of Candia. Such were the conditions when the Senate invited applications for the post of *bailo*. The successful candidate was a certain

---

[1] Every Embassy at Constantinople has—or had—a Turkish speaking "dragoman," who conducted all verbal conversations with the Turkish Ministers besides acting as an expert adviser on Turkish affairs. The word "dragoman" is a corruption of the Turkish word *terguman*, meaning interpreter.   [2] *Viaggi a Constantinopoli* printed at Venice in 1687.

Senator Donado, who was singled out "for his nobility of birth, loftiness of mind, firmness of character and opulent wealth." Donado at once set to work to collect a staff including secretaries, professors of medicine and surgery respectively, dragomans (of whom Benetti was one) and a spiritual adviser. Meanwhile the Turkish Government were asked to send an escort to conduct the new representative through Turkish territory to his post. The escort, accompanied by a dragoman of the Porte, duly arrived at the end of October, but Donado considering the season too advanced for so long a journey, postponed his departure till the following year.

When the mild spring weather came preparations were made for the start and a frigate named the "Dove," equipped with all manner of provisions, lay anchored off the Lido ready to transport the party to Spalato which was then the usual starting place for overland travellers to Constantinople. The Pope sent an autograph letter wishing Donado God-speed, the Doge and his brother-senators gave him a formal farewell and after taking leave of his numerous friends the ambassador-designate was fetched from his palace in a decorated barge flying the standard of Saint Mark and, accompanied down the Grand Canal by a countless fleet of gondolas, was rowed in state aboard his ship. The "Dove" weighed anchor the following day and after coasting safely down the Dalmatian shore, landed her passengers at Spalȧto.

Having solemnly received the Holy Sacrament for the last time before leaving Christian soil, the little band set out on their journey through the Balkans. They were protected by a squadron of Turkish horse and lodged on the road at the common *khans*, where the proud Venetian Senator kept up a dignified exclusiveness by living behind a shelter of canvas screens.

The chief incident of the journey occurred near Belgrade where they came upon a wounded fellow countryman who had been robbed and stripped by brigands and left half-dead on the road. The rescued man proved to be a Roman by birth who at the tender age of ten had been captured by the Turks together with his uncle, a Knight of Malta. The knight had died in the Galleys, but the boy was made to renounce his faith and became the slave of a Turkish *agha*. He regained his freedom on his master's death and at once renouncing Islam had started off for his native land, only to fall into the brigands' hands *en route*. The unlucky man was treated by the embassy surgeon and being restored to health was admitted a member of the suite.

Two months after leaving the Adriatic, Donado and his party reached their destination and entering Stambul by the Ayoub Gate, crossed the Golden Horn and took up their quarters in the ancient *bailaggio*. A striking phenomenon which occurred at the moment of their arrival fills several pages of the diary. An enormous comet stretching across more than a quarter of the firmament appeared in the Northern sky and evoked the wildest speculations among the superstitious inhabitants. Each of the many races living within the walls of Stambul had its own astrologers and these had each his own interpretations of the celestial portent. Benetti was somewhat entertained by the divergence of their views. The Turks—who may have already scented the coming turn of events—declared that the comet sweeping from East to West foretold the onward march of Turkish conquest in Europe. The Jews, true to their racial trait, gave it a religious significance and discerned in it a sign of the Messiah's coming birth; the Persian colony augured a revival of their country's power and the recovery of Bagdad; while the opportunist Greeks loudly proclaimed it a token from heaven against the Roman church and a solemn warning from God to the Pope to renounce his heresy and make submission to the Patriarch.

Shortly after his arrival, the new *bailo* "took over" from his predecessor, who left for Venice after having, as a noble parting act, ransomed a dozen Christian slaves from the *bagno* to take home in his ship. The succeeding year passed with little of interest for the diarist to note. In the following August (1682) the ambassador presented his credentials amid the scenes described already in the previous chapter, and he gained meanwhile a firm foot-hold by winning the gratitude and friendship of Mushib Pasha, Mohammed's favourite son-in-law, who was cured of a ten years' lameness by Dr Tilli, the Pisan surgeon attached to the embassy.

In the same month as the audience an event took place which put all the foreign embassies in the greatest flutter. The horse-tails were set up in the courtyard of the Palace. This was the call to arms and, like the fiery cross in old Scottish days, the signal spread rapidly through the length and breadth of the land, so that within a week or two every pasha from Epirus to the Persian Gulf had received the news and planted his own horse-tail as a rallying point for the troops of his province.

But with all this open preparation for war the enemy was yet to seek. No breach had occurred with any Christian State and Donado and his fellow diplomats

Pleuianders luytants.

TURKISH WRESTLING

From Nicolay's *Pérégrinations faictes en la Turquie,* 1577

were kept on tenterhooks not knowing on which of their countries the blow was to fall. All their attempts to probe the Sultan's secret were in vain and they could only report home that every night thousands of troops and masses of supplies and ammunition were passed across the Bosphorus, but what their destination was no one could tell.

This condition of affairs lasted for several months, during which time the Sultan hid his intentions, whatever they were, under a veil of forced frivolity. First a great regatta was held in front of one of his waterside palaces on the Bosphorus, Mohammed himself looking on from a balcony while the embassy party boarded one of their own merchantmen, which was moored near the spot. A suspicious ruse attempted on this occasion increased the Venetian's apprehensions. A message arrived from the Sultan asking that the captain of the ship should favour the Turks with an exhibition of naval drill and Venetian fighting tactics. The trick was a little too obvious and the wily ambassador had an answer returned that his countrymen never fought in narrow waters and the Bosphorus was not wide enough to give scope for their regular manœuvres.

There were also games, wrestling and *jerid* throwing on the At Maidan, the Hippodrome of old Byzantine days. The last was a Turkish form of tilting and the favourite sport of the palace pages. Benetti describes how the players divided into two "sides" of twenty or thirty each and drew up facing each other across the *maidan*. Then a champion from one of the ranks would ride out, poising his *jerid* (a short wooden staff), dash across the space and turning sharply in front of the opposite line hurl his weapon at the head of one of his opponents. The latter was either knocked off his horse, or, if he successfully dodged the blow, rode out in turn and chased his assailant trying to unhorse him. While the pursuit continued, two more players would issue from the original line and attack in the same fashion, followed by a team of three and so forth till both sides were locked in a general *mêlée*. No protection was worn and the *jerids* being of stout dimensions there were broken heads galore ; in fact it was no uncommon thing, as we learn from other writers, for a player to be knocked dead on the spot.

A much more placid form of entertainment was provided by a friendly pasha who invited Donado and his dragoman out to his country seat at Ayoub, a pretty village on the Sweet Waters of Europe. They found a meal spread in an Italian Garden built in terraces up a hill side with a beautiful view down the Golden Horn. Magnificent tulips—some, Benetti assures us, growing three or four on a stem—anemones of every colour imported from Crete and many other flowers filled the beds, while in a delicate *loggia* near the water they were shown a peculiar floral confection (borrowed, one suspects, from the Persians) which consisted of a pyramid constructed in tiers on each of which stood a row of vases of flowers arranged in different colours with a specially selected blossom placed on the apex to crown the whole. They dined *al fresco* on all manner of luxuries including even the forbidden liquor, though Benetti is careful to mention their host's request that they should not spill a drop of wine for fear of polluting his garden.

During this time of suspense the great *hajj* started for Mecca and Dr Antonio crossed over to Scutari to see the pilgrims start. For some days previously the "holy carpet," which the Caliph sends yearly to be spread on the Kaaba, had been lying in state in its carved wooden box in the mosque at Beshiktash. When the day arrived it was closed, sealed with the imperial cypher and loaded on the sacred camel which was to carry it over its 1500 mile journey. The *imam* who led the camel and was destined never to leave its side till Mecca was reached ferried his charge across the Bosphorus to the place of assembly. As they passed through the streets the people hung garlands round the beast's neck and strewed flowers in its path wishing it luck for the journey. The *Hajjis*, flocking from the *khans* where they had been lodging, collected at the appointed spot and formed up to take the road. In front of the carpet marched a military band and a mob of yelling dervishes, together with the "pasha of the pilgrimage" with royal letters to all and sundry to help the pilgrims on their way; behind came the pilgrims themselves old and young, rich and poor, some on horses, most on foot and a few infirm old men in carts, even little children unable to walk riding on their fathers' shoulders. In accordance with the kindly eastern custom a multitude of friends and relatives accompanied the pilgrims to their first night's halting place to speed them on their way, returning on the morrow to the capital.

While the gathering of the army on the shore of Marmora near Silivri was proceeding apace, Mohammed started yet another diversion to distract attention. He is known to history as Mohammed Avji—Mohammed the Hunter—and on this occasion he lived up to his name by organizing a game drive on a quite unparalleled scale. The scene of the drive was the forest of Belgrade which lies close behind Constantinople. Thirty thousand men were impressed to round up the game in an enormous circle at the centre of which kiosks were erected for Mohammed and his favourite wife. The work of narrowing the circle lasted for fifteen days during which time several hundreds of the wretched beaters, who were flogged mercilessly into the thickets and jungles, died of hunger and exhaustion, and this was in spite of the fact that a special tax had been levied throughout the European vilayets to provide funds for the occasion, the yield of the tax having as usual remained in the pockets of the palace officials. The " bag " from this monstrous drive was frankly pitiable—a leopard, six ibex and a few dozen hares. The total kill included, in fact, many more human beings than beasts.

At last by May 1683 the army was ready to march and, further concealment being useless, the Sultan, egged on as always by Black Mustafa, arranged for a spectacular show to popularize the campaign. The camp at Silivri contained by now many thousands of men, representing the levies from Asiatic Turkey including Mesopotamia. On one flank was the Sultan's private camp, a vast enclosure more than a quarter of a mile in circumference shut in by screens and containing within it an enormous tent in three compartments, one of which served as a throne room, as well as a hall of justice, domed Turkish baths with fountains laid on and a hundred other extravagances. The Grand Vizir was camped near by in almost equal luxury and the army itself occupied a large well-watered valley, where the countless variegated tents of red, green, white and orange presented a wonderful sight.

The favourite Sultana travelled out to see the

spectacle and Benetti was fortunate enough to see her start from her palace on the Bosphorus. Little could, it is true, be seen of the lady herself as she was shielded from the public gaze by a double line of black eunuchs holding hangings of green silk above the level of her head. The same eunuchs formed a human curtain round her as she sat in her *caïque*, which the Bostanji Bashi steered standing with averted face in the stern. Crowds of *bostanjis* lined the banks as the *caïque* passed on its way to Stambul and according to custom handfuls of silver were thrown to them whenever the boat came near the shore. From Stambul the Sultana drove out to visit the camp in a cart drawn by four horses harnessed abreast and with all the usual iron work replaced by silver.

Finally Mohammed himself made a royal progress to the camp. The scene must have been one of the most magnificent that even Constantinople, that city of splendours, had ever seen. I cannot do better than give the picture just as Benetti describes it.

At the head of the procession went the Prophet's green standard borne by an emir with a dervish by his side shouting "huwa, huwa" (*i.e.* "He! He!" a periphrase for God); more dervishes in hair coats, preachers of the *jehad*, followed him. Then came the Stambul Effendi and the two Cadiaskers (the highest judicial officers) wearing turbans of such a size that a man's arms could hardly embrace them. Then the Grand Mufti (the Primate of Islam) in plain white. Then some *ichoghlans* leading wolf-hounds in gold-embroidered coats and red spiked collars, and four horsemen carrying hunting leopards on their saddles. Two plumed camels came next, one carrying the Koran in a green case, the

other a piece of cloth from the Prophet's tomb wrapt
in a gold cover. After these a *chorbaji* with 100 janissaries marching by twos and carrying their cauldrons,
who had with them their cooks in black leather aprons
and their *sakkas,* or water carriers, riding on belaurelled
horses. Next 100 *saimens,* the Sultan's archer bodyguard, in their peculiar helmets of beaten gold, followed
by *dellis* in tiger and panther skins, and detach-
ments of Bosnians and Tartars. Next an important
Pasha with a white martingale on his horse made of
plaited hairs from the tail of the Prophet's own
steed.

Next 150 pikemen (a late introduction into the
Turkish army) in mail with green and yellow cloaks
worn plaidwise over their shoulders, their horses also in
armour, with metal plates on flanks, shoulders and rump,
and gay with fringed velvet saddle-cloths, bridles a-
jingle with little gold plaques, and twisted coloured reins.
Then four silk banners with an escort of 80 *aghas.* Then
a dozen *chaoushes* carrying black staves hung about
with little silver chains. Then the massed "tails" of
the Sultan himself, the Grand Vizir and the principal
pashas ; white horse-tails these were, mounted on red
poles with silver balls on the top. Next came the Grand
Vizir preceded by a band of horsemen with kettle drums,
pipers, cymbal-players and trumpeters (military bands,
one may observe, are said to have originated with the
Turks). He was followed by a group of the palace
pages resplendent in shining mail with caps plastered
with gold disks and twined around with green and red
silks.

Immediately behind them rode Mohammed in person,
a dazzling figure in a white "toga" with gold-embroidered

AN OFFICER OF JANISSARIES

From Nicolay's *Pérégrinations faictes en la Turquie*, 1577

flowers and frogs composed of brilliants; a fur-lined hood hung on his back and he wore on his head the narrow turban with a diamond spray which was part of the imperial insignia. The man himself was a sad contrast to his magnificent trappings as he rode along with bent shoulders, his peaked nose, thin beard, scraggy neck and undistinguished features relieved only by the fine black eyes which were the heirloom of the imperial house. The *Shahzadeh* (the Crown Prince), a fine young man of 18, rode behind his father, and after him came more pages including the *silihdar* with the sultan's sword and the turban-valet with two of the royal turbans. Six coachfuls of *sultanas* came next, the first of them, containing the favourite wife, drawn by eight white ponies, the others by six. The vehicles were covered with rounded hoods painted in arabesques and curtained in red and green. Other ladies of the harem followed in horse-litters and a score of buffalo carts carried members of their households. A regiment of *spahis* and the royal corps of tent-pitchers with twenty camels loaded with carpets and other furniture of the camp brought up the rear.

In and out of the procession as it passed along ran a number of excited dervishes, naked except for their little green aprons fringed with beads of ebony, but wearing the towering Persian hat of brown camel's hair peculiar to their order. Their business was to stir up the troops to a religious ferment, which they did with fanatical cries and deafening blasts on cow-horns.

When the Sultan had joined the troops at Silivri the nervous apprehensions of the foreign ambassadors were tenfold increased. It was clear that an attack on an unprecedented scale was on the point of being launched against some Christian Power, for besides the army encamped near the capital such enormous numbers of *spahis* had crossed the Bosphorus and marched on towards Adrianople that it was clear that every pasha, *sanjak* and *bey* in Asia had obeyed the summons. At the same time naval preparations were going ahead, all the old galleys being overhauled and many new ones built. Each representative used his powers of diplomatic persuasion to head off the Turk from his own country and encourage an attack on his neighbour, and the prospect looked black for the case of Venice when news arrived of a deplorable fracas at Zara where a number of Dalmatians had risen against their Turkish masters, killed the *sanjak's* brother, massacred some hundreds of Turks and pillaged and burnt the *aghas'* homesteads. On hearing this dire report Donado at once asked for another audience, but the Sultan being now in his camp refused to see any foreign envoy on the typical pretext that his dignity would be sullied by sitting on the tent floor on the same level as a Christian. At this point, however, the friendship of Mushib stood the ambassador in good stead. Through his agency he managed to induce the *Mufti* to issue a *fetva* to the effect that the Zara outrage was not a *casus belli*. A week later the secret was out. Vienna was the Turkish objective and the troops were to march at once. The German and Polish ambassadors received instructions to accompany the army; the "subject" envoys of Ragusa, Transylvania, Moldavia and Wallachia had to go too; the French, British and Venetian representatives determined to remain at the capital.

The day before the start a terrific storm swept across Constantinople and wrought dire confusion in the camp.

All the tents were levelled and the streams coming down in spate flooded the valley, drowned men and beasts, ruined a large part of the stores and reduced the Sultan's sumptuous quarters to a pulp. This in itself was a bad enough omen, but what really devastated the minds of the Turks was the seemingly trivial occurrence of the Sultan's turban being blown off his head by a gust of wind. From this moment popular confidence in the success of the war was badly shaken and Black Mustafa, who was known for its real author, became the object of the people's hate.

The ambitious Vizir, could not, however, be daunted by an accident of nature and he persuaded the Sultan to lead out the army as soon as the damage was repaired. Though the streams were still almost impassable and a special carriage with 6-foot wheels drawn by twelve horses had to be made to transport the Sultan across country, on April 7th, 1682 the troops marched out, the Janissaries defiling according to custom in front of their *agha* and presenting him with baskets of fruit and flowers as they passed.

With the Turkish army went Mushib Pasha accompanied by Dr Tilli, the embassy surgeon, whose letters written to Benetti *en route* and reproduced in the latter's diary tell of some of the features of the great march. The rains which had made such havoc of the Silivri camp continued to fall and so sodden was the country that the troops, spreading out to avoid the trodden ground, churned a track four miles wide across the plains. On reaching Belgrade the Sultan handed over command to the Grand Vizir consigning the Prophet's standard to him in the presence of the troops. He took up his own residence in the town and settled down with his wives and household to pursue his usual life of pleasure. Hunts were held in the surrounding country and a fleet of *caïques* on the Bosphorus model was built to carry the royal party for pleasure trips on the Danube. One of the *fêtes* organized to amuse the Sultan included a sort of Lord Mayor's procession, and Dr Tilli specially mentions a freakish and rather gruesome item invented by a Persian servant of one of the pashas. A cart paraded through the streets bearing what to all appearance was the dismembered trunk of a man with his head severed and lying apart from the body. Although seemingly decapitated and wallowing in gore, the body breathed and occasionally moved its position to the intense stupefaction of the on-lookers. The surgeon's scientific curiosity was naturally aroused by such an incredible phenomenon and he tracked the mystery to its source, only to find that this early exponent of Mr Maskelyn's art had concocted the scene with the help of five separate men protruding different parts of their anatomy from under a black cloth and a liberal splashing of red paint!

The army meanwhile began to suffer from the inevitable defects of its enormous size, and the commissariat threatened to break down, the lack of bread becoming so severe that the janissaries actually raided the Grand Vizir's own bakery. Many of the guns moreover became bogged through the persistent bad weather and the spirits of the troops were badly damped by the news that Poland was preparing to join forces with their old enemy Austria to repel the Turks.

At Constantinople, however, enthusiasm ran high and on the day that news arrived of the crossing of the Raab the deputy *Mufti* ordered a day of prayer and thanksgiving. The morning service in the mosques was attended by the children from every school in the capital and after it was over the congregations formed up outside in columns of two each led by an *imam*. The processions marching from the various mosques met on the At Maidan where temporary pulpits had been erected beforehand. Here the whole immense assembly prayed towards Mecca and were afterwards addressed by a number of preachers who enjoined prayer and fasting, abstention from all vices and constant warfare on behalf of Islam, urging the hearers to risk martyrdom for the sake of the faith and to fight for pure religion and not for worldly profit. Having listened to these admirable sentiments from the lips of the *hojas*, the crowd departed in profound silence broken only by the chanting of *suras* from the Koran. The populace were not content, however, with these religious performances, but vented their exuberance in an outburst of jollification which bore a singular resemblance to our modern celebrations; the whole town was illuminated, fireworks were discharged in the open spaces, guns fired from the Topkhaneh and effigies of Christian princes, bishops, cardinals and the Pope himself were carried about the streets and then burnt.

In the midst of these celebrations the report came of the death of the Sultan-Valida (the Turkish Queen Mother) which had taken place at Adrianople. Messengers were sent out at once to spread the news through the empire and special envoys were sent with alms to Mecca. The body had been partially embalmed and placed in a wooden coffin packed with ice which was loaded on a cart and brought at the trot (an unusual pace for these cumbersome Turkish vehicles) to the capital,

followed by a string of carriages full of the deceased
lady's servants. At the city gate the cart was met by
such of the Ministers of State as had remained behind
when the army left and the coffin, draped with coloured
silks and tissue of gold, was carried on their shoulders
through the town followed by a great multitude of
mourners including a host of indigent females who
had lived on the charitable Sultana's bounty. The procession went at the rapid pace customary at Eastern
funerals till they reached the mosque which the Sultan-
Valida had built in her life-time to accommodate her
remains, and there was left in the little domed chamber
made for it, the *imam* of the mosque having first spread
it with a green embroidered cloth and placed a turban
at its head.

It was not long before the blow fell which was to
turn Constantinople from joy to mourning. For some
weeks after the investment of Vienna had begun there
was a complete stoppage of news from the front. One
day a solitary *spahi* arrived breathless with the news
that Vienna had fallen and a fresh outburst of jubilation
took place, while the carrier of the good tidings was
fêted by everyone and loaded with presents. Next day
the *spahi* had disappeared and the people of Stambul
realized that they had been duped. A few days later it
was known that the Grand Vizir's army, after taking
the outer forts and all but breaking the Christian line,
had been fallen upon unexpectedly by Sobiesky and
had fled in disorder. Presently the fugitives began to
arrive. They had poured back through the Balkans in
utter confusion committing horrible atrocities on the
way, murdering the Christian rayahs and burning their
houses to warm themselves at night. When the Asiatic

soldiery reached the shore of the Bosphorus the Bostanji Bashi, who had charge of the small craft, tried to prevent their crossing, but the threat to the capital itself became so great that it was decided to let them go over.

The Sultan meanwhile had left Belgrade upholding the tradition of his house by refusing to admit the slightest recognition of defeat. He marched out of the town with a double band playing before him, having continued his huntings and junketings to the last. One symptom of his true feelings he gave, namely to order a St Bartholomew's massacre of all the Christians at Constantinople and that the foreign envoys in particular should be sliced into small pieces. Fortunately for Donado and his colleagues the Grand Mufti dissuaded Mohammed from carrying out this drastic measure, pointing out that it was no moment for adding to the number of Turkey's enemies abroad.

Before leaving Constantinople Donado successfully fulfilled his mission by getting the Sultan's signature to a new treaty of amity and commerce with the Serene Republic. He had asked the Senate to relieve him of his post after the severe strain of the last two years and a successor having been appointed, he made his arrangements to return to Venice. The route he had come by was now impossible as the whole of the country was seething with rapine and anarchy owing to the flood of deserters from the army, so he again had recourse to the goodwill of Mushib who provided the party with a vessel to take them home by sea. A Turkish admiral who was just then sailing for Candia was ordered to take the Venetians' ship under his charge as far as Crete as there was grave danger from corsairs. One little *contretemps* occurred before they were clear of the

Bosphorus, the current having driven the ship ashore where the bows made havoc of the stucco façade of a pasha's palace. The incident, though slight, seemed likely to have serious consequences in the then irritated state of public feeling, but harm was happily averted by the renewed good offices of the Sultan's son-in-law.

When Constantinople had at length been left behind and the two ships had passed the Dardanelles, Donado's first care was to give the slip to his escort, reckoning that a revengeful Turkish admiral might well be a worse danger than any corsair to a defenceless shipload of Christians. He therefore stole away at night and navigating the ship himself brought her safely to Suda Bay, one of the three diminutive possessions which his countrymen still maintained in Crete. After a cordial reception by the *Proveditore* and the small Venetian garrison and a stay of several days which the enterprising senator devoted to spying out the Turkish defences of Canea, the party put to sea again and, joining forces with the great Morosini who had been cruising in the neighbouring waters, arrived safely home again in the first week of June 1684.

CHAPTER XIII

A BELATED CRUSADE

The following story of a forlorn hope undertaken by a company of French gentlemen against the Turk in Crete has come down to us in a little book published in 1669 by a bookseller of Grenoble into whose hands the diary of a member of the expedition happened to fall.

The event itself took place in the previous year, the twenty-first year of the siege of Candia, and to make the circumstances more intelligible it may be well to take a glance back over Cretan history. The island, when the Turks began to threaten it, had enjoyed Christian rule ever since the days of Constantine the Great, except for a brief possession by the Arabs in the caliphate of Harun er-Rashid. The Venetian occupation dated back to 1207 when the Republic secured the island in a rather curious manner. As a part of the Byzantine empire it had fallen to the leaders of the fourth crusade when they abandoned their campaign against the Saracens and captured Constantinople. Baldwin I, on crowning himself emperor, allotted Crete to one of his subalterns, Boniface, Marquis of Montferrat and "King of Thessalonica," who, finding the property of little use to himself, sold it to Venice for 1000 marks and a portion of territory in Macedonia.

The island had thus been a Venetian colony for

nearly five centuries at the time of its invasion by a
Turkish army in 1644. In that year one of the wives
of the Sultan (the degenerate Ibrahim) happened to be
going on a pilgrimage to Mecca and was sailing past
Crete in a Turkish ship when they met a Venetian
galley which promptly captured the vessel. The sultana
was taken prisoner together with the rest of the
passengers, and this so infuriated the sultan that he
at once declared war on Venice. His first act was to
send his Vizir with an army to Crete under orders to
capture the island. Canea (the modern capital) was
taken almost immediately, Retimo, another of the
three main towns, fell a year later and Candia alone
held out. Into this fortress, behind fortifications so
tremendously solid that—except where intentionally
demolished—they stand intact to this day, the Governor
of the island, Morosini, withdrew with his troops and
endured a siege of twenty years.

Though locked in this fortress on the land, the
Venetians maintained the upper hand on the sea, which
enabled them to keep the garrison supplied with provisions and reinforcements. By 1668, however, their
resources were nearly exhausted; twenty years' warfare
had emptied the treasury almost to the last sequin and
the garrison of Candia, long unrelieved, were clearly
unable to hold out much longer. When things reached
this pass the Pope intervened in the name of religion
and sent a pressing appeal to Louis XIV to assist in
repulsing the infidel. A definite breach with the Turks
was too great a risk for Louis, but he salved his con-
science by privately ordering one of his officers, a
certain M. de la Feuillade, to raise volunteers to go to
the help of the Venetians at Candia in the guise of

private adventurers. Five hundred nobles and gentlemen of France volunteered for the enterprise and in the autumn of the year sailed out from Toulon in ships flying the flag of Malta.

When off the Sardinian coast they found themselves windbound near the bay of Palmas and there met with an adventure which is worthy of mention if only to show how little the inhabitants of that island had advanced from the primitive state by the end of the seventeenth century. A party from the ship going ashore found a number of roughly made skiffs drawn up on rollers near the foot of the cliffs in front of a row of troglodytes' caves. They entered a cave and discovered hanging from the roof a quantity of game which they promptly annexed for their own commissariat. As they were leaving with their plunder, a crowd of "ugly great satyres" emerged from neighbouring caves and set on them with clubs and boulders, trying to head them off from their boat. Luckily their friends of the ship perceived their predicament and an armed crew rowed to the shore just in time to save them from the fury of the despoiled islanders.

Twenty-five days out from Toulon the ship reached Malta, where M. de la Feuillade interviewed the Grand Master and begged him, for the honour of his Order and the Holy Catholic Church, to do what he could to forward the expedition. An appeal for volunteers was answered by nearly all the French knights at Valetta, a fair number of the Germans and Italians and a solitary Spaniard, and with this accession to their force the party sailed on towards Crete.

Thirteen days later they anchored off Standia, an island lying some half-a-dozen miles from Candia and serving the Venetians as a naval base for the island. The same evening their leader was taken to the mainland to confer with General Morosini. The situation which he found on arrival was a very unpleasant shock to his religious ardour. A small French force under the Marquis de Ville had for some time past formed part of the garrison and an important redoubt, the bastion of St André, had been committed to them to defend. But the strain of the interminable siege, added to the jealousy between the two nations, had raised ill-feeling between them to such a pitch that the Venetian commanders had recently made a traitorous and dastardly attempt to get rid of their allies by a secret arrangement with the Turks. The latter were invited to attack the bastion on a certain day when the Venetians were to fire their guns on the Frenchmen from the rear. By a fortunate chance the Marquis de Ville intercepted a letter and learnt of the plot. He kept his own counsel, but made quiet arrangements to embark all his men, and having done so successfully, sailed straight off to Venice and laid his charge before the Senate. The Senate, to save their country's fair name, heavily bribed the Marquis to hush up the matter and sail back to Candia as though nothing had happened. The bribe did its work and the Frenchmen returned to the island shortly before their compatriots arrived on the scene.

The Turks meantime had taken the bastion abandoned by the French and blown it up with gunpowder, thus making a serious breach in the defences and bringing the forces so close to each other that the soldiers could actually touch one another with the ends of their muskets and exchange food and tobacco. As soon as M. de la Feuillade had brought his men into harbour—which he managed to do with very slight loss from the Turkish batteries commanding the entrance —Morosini assigned to them a place in the line near the ruins of St André's bastion.

The new arrivals were full of eagerness for the fray and at once began a series of raids on the Turkish trenches carried out at night by parties of twenty or so armed with grenades, *pôts-à-feu* and other devices for harrying the enemy in his earthworks. Not content with this they presently clamoured for a general sortie. The Venetians' ardour had had time to cool in the long years of the siege, and at first Morosini refused to listen to any suggestion of the sort. The most that M. de la Feuillade managed to extort by importunate pleading was a grudging promise to support the French with the garrison artillery if they chose to conduct an attack "on their own."

The French held a council of war in their camp and it was unanimously carried that sedentary warfare was unworthy of the traditions of the *noblesse de France* and that chivalry demanded more brilliant feats of arms. It was therefore resolved to launch a determined offensive on the part of the Turkish lines opposite their sector of the fortifications. By this time, as a result of disease and casualties in the raids, the numbers of the force had dwindled to barely 450. These, with another 100 men, lent at the last moment by Morosini, attacked at daybreak on December 16th a force of 2500 Turks.

Each man in the attack carried a half-pike and a pair of pistols, swords having proved themselves valueless weapons against the Turkish scimitars. Armour was not worn because of the sultry weather. The odds in favour of the Turks were further enhanced by the fact that they possessed far better muskets than the Christians and were admittedly better shots.

The Venetians refused to allow any gates to be opened to let the attacking party out of the fortress, so the latter were reduced to knocking a hole through the wall large enough to give passage to one man at a time. Creeping through this aperture while it was still dark, they lined up in the "fausse-braye" immediately under the walls and waited for dawn.

The signal for the start was given by a grenade fired from the battlements above, and the attackers at once rushed forward under a heavy fire from the Turkish trenches which, in their turn, were pounded by the Venetian guns. The French crusaders had spent the previous night in prayer and devotion and a religious fervour spurred them on to victory or martyrdom. One of their priests, Père Paul by name, a Capucin monk, took the lead and, with a crucifix held aloft, forged recklessly ahead across the Turkish lines followed by his countrymen. The Turks fought desperately as the Frenchmen forced them back and the slaughter was terrific, the Turkish killed —according to a prisoner captured next day—amounting to twice the total number of their assailants. Reinforcements, however, soon began to pour in from other parts of the line and it became clear that if the advance continued the French force would be cut off beyond hope of retirement. Seeing this, M. de la Feuillade hastened ahead and, catching up Père Paul with the greatest difficulty, succeeded, after addressing "une petite réprimande" to the priest, in checking his wild career and turned his men back towards the fortress. When they began to retire, the Turks, never dreaming that such a handful of men could have dared to attack without strong reserves, and suspecting a trap, held back from pursuing them. Thus the survivors effected their retreat and regained the fortress by the miserable opening through which they had issued.

When the roll was called after the battle only a few score were found to remain of the gallant 500 who had sailed from Toulon and the hundred or so knights who had joined them from Malta. They decided therefore to wait only for some of the wounded to recover before sailing back to France. The war-worn remnant were not put back in the line but spent the interval in the town itself which gave them the chance of observing conditions in Candia.

It was found that the place contained an extraordinarily mixed population. The prospect of Turkey obtaining a foothold so far west as Crete had awakened a glimmer of the old solidarity among the European nations, many of whom, like the French, had sent contingents to help the Venetians in defending the island. Hence the garrison of about 7000 was a most cosmopolitan force including, besides the Venetians and their Greek and Slav subjects, representatives of other Italian States, French, Germans, Swiss, Savoyards and knights of St John of Jerusalem.

The whole of this force, and the native population as well, "fed," as the diarist puts it, "on the bread of St Mark"; in other words, they drew all their provisions from Venice. Rations were consequently exceedingly short and even the wounded in hospital lived chiefly on broth made from bread-crumbs, a diet "not very agreeable to the taste, nor calculated to restore strength to sick men, but a good reducer of fever."

At last in the middle of January M. de la Feuillade re-embarked his men and, choosing a murky night, slipped out of the harbour unharmed by the salvos of cannon-balls with which the Turks sped his departure.

Even now their trials were not over, for being caught in one of the furious storms which habitually rage round Crete, they were driven southward from their course and nearly wrecked on the Barbary coast. No sooner was this peril past than plague broke out on the ship and carried off many of the remaining survivors. Touching again at Valetta, they landed their Maltese friends and then sailed on to Toulon which they reached by the end of February.

Here one of the party, celebrating a *quarantaine* in thankfulness to God for his safe home-coming, employed the leisure it gave him in writing up the diary from which the foregoing pages are borrowed.

The year was not out before Candia fell. Venice then concluded a peace with the Turks, surrendering Crete all but Suda Bay and a couple of second-rate fortresses ; even these were yielded to the Turks in the course of the next few years. It is interesting to note that Francesco Morosini, the defender of Candia, became soon afterwards Doge of Venice.

CHAPTER XIV

A BUNDLE OF GLEANINGS

One of the most entertaining of English writers of
Turkish travels was a certain Dr Covel, Fellow of
Christ's College, Cambridge, and later Vice-Chancellor
of the University. In 1675, when on his way to the
East he found himself a spectator at the circumcision
festivities of a Turkish Prince. The boy, whom Covel
describes as an "ugly ill-favoured chit," was the son of
Sultan Murad III and the ceremony took place at
Adrianople where his father was then in camp.

It was a charitable Turkish custom for a rich man,
when his son was circumcised, to allow a number of
poor boys, whose parents could not afford the cost of a
decent ceremony, to share in the rite. In the case of
princes of the royal blood the fortunate urchins received
afterwards the name of "Prince's pensioners" and drew
three aspers a day for life from the privy purse. Accompanied by a score or so of his future "pensioners" Prince
Mustafa was led on horseback to his father's tent.

As the weather was hot he had men riding on either
side with large fans of Bustard's feathers to fan him
and shelter him from the sun; *sakkas* with water-skins
ran in front sprinkling the road and a corps of *tooloonjis*,
as they were called, kept back the crowd with the aid
of blown-out bladders daubed in tar, from which, the
observant don remarks, "the spruce Turks fly as from
the Divel."

A procession followed in which the most remarkable feature consisted of a number of so-called *nakuls*. These peculiar objects were in somewhat the form of a may-pole, being upright poles with wire cones on the top covered with coloured paper ornaments and little wax flowers and fruits. Two specially large ones, nearly 30 feet high, were supported on frameworks carried by 100 slaves each, whose movements were directed, as though they were the crew of a ship, by a galley-master standing on top and giving blasts on a whistle. When the procession reached the camp the Prince was received with kisses by his father, and the *nakuls*, which served no other purpose than ornament, were planted in front of the tent.

The ceremony was then performed by the Sultan's chief surgeon, an Italian renegade who received as his fee a sum equivalent to £6000 (so, at least, he assured Covel) which was presented to him by the Valida, the prince's mother, in a silver basin.

On the evening of the day a public *fête* was held in front of the camp, and Covel gives an interesting account of the various sports and side-shows, which were sur-prisingly like those at an English fair. First he de-scribes the dancing. The dancers, who in this case were men, wore tights with elaborate girdles and a full petti-coat "of some merry colour" reaching to their ankles. A space was cleared for them into which they came bounding on and forming up in a semicircle performed "wriggling" dances to the accompaniment of castanets; they finished the dance with a giddy twirl and with a bow to the audience bounded off again.

There were pantomimes in which men dressed up as beasts, notably a large deer, "played 1000 freakes" and there were games such as follow-my-leader in which the actors had to copy faithfully the elaborate gestures and grimaces of their captain. The familiar strong man was represented by a *bostanji* who juggled with balls of stone and stood with bare feet on the edges of scimitars; his fellow, having rigged a pulley on some scaffolding and taken a young camel on his shoulders, pulled himself up off the ground by a rope secured to his own hair. An elderly Arab, whom Covel describes as "exceeding black and shrivelled, his head bald and shining like soot and clad like a Dominican," performed the time-honoured trick of producing such objects as snakes and eggs from the onlookers' noses and other parts of their anatomy.

Bear-baiting with mastiffs went on at one spot, wrestling at another and an opera company (imported *en bloc* by the Venetian ambassador to honour the occasion) performed elsewhere.

But the great feature of all was the fireworks, for which the Turks have always had a great affection, though, as with many other inventions which they adopted from their Christian neighbours, they relied on foreigners to supply the technical skill. A Venetian and a Dutchman were the experts on the present occasion, and they seem to have provided a display of which even Mr Brock might be proud. Some of their set pieces were truly wondrous confections. There were enormous figures of giants made of wooden hoops covered with paper, their hollow insides filled with crackers which spurted out of ears, nose and mouth when the machine was fired; movable pyramids hung all over with little dishes of camphor which were all lit at once; paste-board castles spouting fountains of fire;

a small replica of the old Venetian fort at Candia (which had braved a Turkish siege for 20 years) with men concealed inside who let off rockets through the port holes, and—the most wonderful show of all—a mock naval battle between model ships of war which were slung from cross-beams and manœuvred by their crews with the help of running ropes while they fired broadsides of blank cartridge at each other. A wholesale discharge of star rockets brought the *fête* to a finish.

The subject of Turkish festivities brings us to a description given by another writer, of the extravagant sights to be seen at a royal wedding. On the day of the ceremony the Princess rode through the streets of the capital in a silver-plated coach with all the iron work picked out in gold and an awning edged with precious stones. She was drawn by six white horses in harness of gold and silver with jewelled plumes stuck in their brow-bands. There were postilions on the horses and on each side of the coach rode eunuchs scattering largesse to the crowd. The Sultan's presents to his daughter were also paraded through the town. They included a wax model of a garden with birds and beasts, trees and flowers and clockwork fountains and other models in sugar in the forms of peacocks, ostriches, lions, elephants and sundry other beasts. Among the more substantial gifts there were rolls of stuffs, jewelled slippers, gold-framed mirrors, girdles and bracelets, bottles of rare scent, cabinets and dress-boxes, a beautiful sable vest with diamond and ruby buttons, and finally a team of thirty mules loaded with little painted chests full of bullion and a complete household staff of janissaries.

The writer mentions that one of the events in the sports held to celebrate the wedding was the feat of a

TURKISH FIREWORKS

From George Sandys' *Travels*, 1632

man who walked up a rope stretched from the ground to the top of one of the minarets of Sultan Selim's mosque, down which he afterwards slid with a boy on his shoulders hanging by his hair from a pulley.

A Turkish trait which most of the old writers refer to is their kindness to animals. Anyone who knew Constantinople in the days before the great massacre of the street dogs will remember how Turkish households would adopt and feed families of these mangey brutes, and an amusing example of this soft-heartedness of the people of Stambul towards the brute creation is given by a writer who visited the town rather more than two hundred years ago.

"It is customary," he says, "among Turks to boil and bake paunches, lights, livers and pieces of meat and carry them in wooden buckets up and down the City crying out 'Cats Meat.' The Turks buy the food and give it to the Cats who sit on the walls for they imagine that they obtain especial favour in the eyes of God by giving alms even to irrational cattle, cats, dogs, fish, birds and other live creatures; and therefore they consider it a great sin to kill and destroy captured birds, and prefer to ransome them with money and release them. They throw bread to fishes and give food to cats and dogs at definite times and places. The cats breakfast in good time in the morning and assemble for the second time at the hour of the evening meal in large bodies out of the whole City.

"We went purposely to these walls, listened to their caterwauling and with great laughter watched how they ran out of the houses and assembled. So, too, we saw Turkish Matrons and old women buying pieces of meat on the spit from the kitchen boys and handing them on a long wand to the cats, muttering meanwhile a kind of Turkish prayer,"

Another English writer mentions that birds were always allowed to feed as much as they liked from the great granaries, several thousand dollars a year being written off the accounts to balance their depredations. The birds in Turkey being never molested, were so tame that, he adds, "I have thrown my coat over turtle doves in the highways, and quails would ordinarily hop upon our legs and arms as we slept in the fields."

The natural charitableness of the Turk found another outlet in the erection by wealthy men of hospices all over the country for the benefit of wayfarers. Lodging was *gratis* and any genuine traveller, be he Turk, Jew, infidel or heretic, was allowed to rest for three days on end in any of these *khans*, during which time he had the use of a room to sleep in and a generous ration of bread, rice and honey. Some of the larger hostels, built for a great part by members of the imperial family, had accommodation for a thousand guests.

These monuments of charity were in such strange contrast with the brutality towards the subject races of Turkey that Blunt compares them to "daintie fruits growing on a Dunghill." As outward signs of subservience to their conquerors, Ottoman Christians had to paint their houses black, wear nothing but black clothes and when riding, dismount whenever they met a Moslem. Christian travellers from foreign countries, on the other hand, were seldom molested if they walked circumspectly and studiously avoided offending against native susceptibilities in manners or dress.

An English traveller remarks that "if ever I appeared clothed in the least part like an Englishman, I was tufted like an Owle among birds. This I at first imputed to Barbarism but on lamenting thereof to a Turk of the better sort, he told me his nation would stand no novelties and therefore disgraced all new examples; so that I perceived it to be rather a piece of Institution than any incivilitie." As a practical instance he tells the following story.

"I clad in Turkish manner was riding with two Turks an hour ahead of the caravan. We found four Spahi Timariots by a river where we stayed; they were at dinner and seeing by my head I was a Christian they called to me. I not understanding what they would, stood still till they menacing their weapons, rose and came to m'e with looks very ugly. I smilingly met them and taking him who seemed of most port by the hand layed it to my forehead, which with them is the greatest sign of love and honour. Then, often calling him *Sultanum*, spoke English which, though none of the kindest, gave I it such a sound as to them who understood no further might seem affectionate, humble and hearty. This so appeased them as they made me sit and eat and we parted lovingly; presently after, they met the Caravan where was a Ragusan merchant of quality. He being clothed in the Italian fashion and spruce, they justled him and he not yet considering how the place had changed his condition, stood upon his terms till they with their axes and iron maces broke two of his ribs, in which case we left him behind half-dead either to get back as he could or be devoured of beasts."

A danger from which foreigners in Turkey were never quite free was that of being seized by a chance Turk, usually a Janissary, and sold as a slave to the first slave buyer. Indeed the author of the last quotations mentions that on one occasion he was attacked by a sort of press-gang who tried to hustle him into a house, presumably for this purpose, and was only saved by using his knife.

In spite of the barriers which the Turks set up against their Christian fellows, they were, on the whole, not a fanatical nation. To show how tolerant even a religious functionary could be on occasion, I will repeat a story told by an amusing French artist named Grelot who visited Constantinople in the latter half of the 17th century to make drawings of its principal buildings and other features, which he published with a dedication to Louis XIV in 1680.

In order to sketch the interior of Santa Sofia, Grelot had to arrange for admission to the galleries under the great dome. He first approached a Greek jeweller of his acquaintance who kept a shop in the mosque precincts and was introduced by him to one of the *kandil-agassis*, or lamp-trimmers. With the help of a cheap watch, bought for the occasion from his friend the jeweller, Grelot overcame any scruples of the lamp-trimmer about allowing a Christian into the mosque for so doubtful a purpose as sketching, and the next day, dressed *à la turque* and wearing a long false beard, he was smuggled in. Each day he entered before sunrise, spent the day hidden in a dark corner of the gallery and emerged again after sunset and continued to do so until he completed an elaborate set of sketches, suffering no greater inconvenience than that of having to meet frequent demands for further *bakhshish* from his accomplice the lamp-trimmer. But on the very last day he was seized with a mischievous desire to play a trick on the Mohammedans by committing a shocking act of sacrilege

STA SOFIA

From Grelot's *Voyage de Constantinople*, 1680

unknown to the worshippers in the mosque. So he bought a bologna sausage and a bottle of wine and, having smuggled them into his usual nook in the gallery, sat down, after finishing his drawing, to a hearty meal. To his unutterable horror just as he had cut up his sausage and was raising the bottle to his lips an elderly Turk appeared round a corner of the gallery. He hastily stuffed his papers in his pockets, bundled sausage and bottle under his skirts and fell into the posture of a moslem at prayer. The Turk came up and told him that the door of the gallery was about to be shut and he must descend at once. The wretched Frenchman, unable to move without discovering the damning relics of his meal, had already resigned himself to a horrible death when the Turk burst into a roar of laughter and told him that he had witnessed his performance from the start, strongly advising him to avoid such foolishness in the future. He then revealed himself as a mosque official who was party to the plot for admitting Grelot to the building and a sharer, of course, in the bribes extorted by the *kandil-agassi*.

It is Grelot again who tells the story of a dervish who sought and obtained from the *imam* of a mosque in the outskirts of the city permission to spend his nights praying in the sanctuary. The dervish belonged to a poor and ascetic order and was very lean and emaciated. His nightly vigils appeared to do him good, for he soon grew better favoured and by the end of a month showed positive signs of plumpness. Meantime the *imam* had more than once been surprised and annoyed by the sudden extinction of some of the lamps which, as is usual in Turkish mosques, hung in large numbers on chains from the roof. At a late hour one night he happened to enter the mosque to see to their filling, and there was the dervish sitting on the ground with three or four lamps around him—safe as he thought from censorious eyes—and enjoying an excellent repast of hunks of bread soaked in olive oil!

The story can the more easily be credited as many of the Turkish dervishes were, like their cousins the friars, most accomplished hypocrites. Nicholas de Nicolay, *géographe ordinaire* to Charles IX of France, who travelled for many years through Turkey collecting data of every description for his royal master, has left a description of the various dervish orders flourishing in his day.

One, which he calls "Geomailers" (an unrecognizable title) consisted, he writes, of gay young men whose sole ambition in taking their vows was to see the world in jolly company and at other peoples' expense. They journey about, he says, singing amatory songs to the accompaniment of cymbals and making love to all the ladies they meet. Their only garment is a short tunic of purple, bound with a silken sash ending in a tassel of bells; they have bells again round their legs fastened below the knee like garters, and they sometimes wear a lion skin over their shoulders with the forelegs knotted in front. They take pride in their hair, which they wear excessively long, even twining in portions of goat's hair (the long-haired Angora variety, of course) to increase its natural length.

To the Calenders he gives a better character as sincere and devout ascetics; but a third order, whom he calls simply "dervis," he describes in anything but flattering terms. They spend the winter, he says, in their *tekyés* but during the summer they range the

A "GEOMAILER"

From Nicolay's *Pérégrinations faictes en la Turquie*, 1577

country committing "mechancetés et volleries" under the aegis of sanctity. They will rob any one they meet and with the hatchet which they carry in their belts they are ready to crack in the skull of a lonely traveller on the smallest possible excuse.

As for their appearance, he adds that they shave the whole head, brand their foreheads with irons, wear jasper earrings and dress in a pair of sheepskins worn one down the back and the other on the chest and tied together down the sides. Often members of this order would catch wild creatures, such as wolves, bears, eagles and stags, and lead them about with bells round their necks as evidence that they had renounced the world and adopted the life of the beasts of the field.

To turn to another subject, the art of witchcraft has at all times been abominated by the Turks. *A propos* of this an old French traveller relates that on landing once at Gallipoli he found quite a colony of sorceresses, mostly Jewish, who compounded love-potions, sold charms and worked magic. They were careful however to practise their trade in secret, for the *chorbaji* was always on the watch and anyone apprehended in witchcraft was at once put in a sack and thrown into the straits.

Superstition, on the other hand, was by no means foreign to the Turk and there is a rather curious case referred to in more than one of the old travel books. Briefly told the facts are as follows. At a place called Kerch in Asia Minor there existed a well of magical healing powers. Round the well lived a peculiar species of birds of a largish size and red and black plumage which were called "Mohammed's fowls." These birds made their principal diet off locusts and attacked them so vigorously whenever they appeared that a plague of the insects would be entirely devoured in a few hours. This trait in the birds was of course invaluable in a part of the world where locusts abound. But the birds—and here comes the superstition—had another peculiarity of their own which seriously diminished their usefulness; they could only live in the vicinity of water from the miraculous well. A single drop of the water was sufficient, but in its absence they slowly languished and died. It is related that the locust plague was especially bad in Cyprus and for years the Cypriots regularly lost the greater part of their crops. At last they chanced to hear of Mohammed's fowls and sent a mission to the remote Anatolian village. They were allowed to take a pitcher of the water and returned with it, followed by several of the birds. The pitcher was carefully lodged on the top of a tower in the middle of the island and for some generations the birds and the crops flourished. Then one year the former suddenly vanished. The anxious Cypriots went to their tower and examined the pitcher; it had sprung a leak and was dry.

The practice of medicine, like most of the sciences, was limited almost entirely to Greeks and other Christians. The Turks indeed have always credited Christians with peculiar powers of healing derived, they believe, by transmission from Christ Himself, whom Mohammedans recognize, as the reader probably knows as one of the greatest of the "prophets." The consequence is that a person who is both a Christian and a recognized doctor commands very great confidence and a large clientèle.

As an instance we have the story—told by M. Tournefort, another geographer royal—of an Irish surgeon who, after serving in the wars in France, went out to Turkey attached to the French Ambassador to the Porte. Their ship touched at Crete some years after the conquest of the island by Turkey, and it happened that a new Viceroy had just arrived, one Ali Pasha an ex-Grand Vizer, suffering from a grievous distemper. On greeting the Ambassador the first thing he asked him was to lend him the services of his surgeon, so our Irish friend went ashore to do what he could to relieve him. He examined his patient and, diagnosing his trouble, popped him into a "powdering-tub."

I am entirely ignorant of the properties of this antique apparatus but the treatment seems to have been drastic, for when at the height of his "salivation" the Pasha concluded he was dying and summoned his Council to decide on a punishment for the surgeon. The Council wisely advised that having made a beginning of the cure he should carry it through to the end and suspend sentence on the surgeon in the meantime. This he grudgingly consented to do and presently, the inflammation subsiding, he emerged from the treatment cured. The Irishman was suitably rewarded with a dress of honour and other presents, but he had little peace during the rest of his stay in Candia for every sick *agha* in the island flocked to his powdering tub and he was, as M. Tournefort puts it, "tired out of his life anointing Musulmans."

CHAPTER XV

A PRISONER IN THE GALLEYS AND THE BLACK TOWER

(1)

Of all the grim fates which could befall a Christian gentleman in the sixteenth century none assuredly could exceed for sheer horror captivity in the hands of the Turks. Nor was it the remote danger which it might easily seem. The Turkish fleet, one must remember, was manned to a very great extent by Christian prisoners, some—and many Englishmen among them—captured from merchant vessels in the Mediterranean, others ordinary prisoners of war. Their total number at any given moment would have amounted to several thousands; and the possibility of capture by the Turks entered sufficiently into the calculations of the men of that day to lead Luther to publish a little manual of advice for Protestant soldiers who might fall into Turkish hands.

We have already read Busbequius's account of the melancholy scene when the remnants of a whole Christian fleet were towed into the Golden Horn and the men taken off into thraldom, and there is hardly a writer of those days who does not refer to the miserable plight of his fellow countrymen languishing in the galleys or in the terrible "Black Tower" which stood at the Eastern mouth of the Bosphorus. Many are their stories of ransomings or escapes. Sandys tells the history of

Hadrian Cant, a Dutchman who escaped from the Tower and was smuggled by the English ambassador home to Holland while the Agha of the Tower, taking warning of the fate of his predecessor who in similar circumstances was "gauched," arranged a mock funeral and lowered a coffin full of stones and clay to the bottom of the Bosphorus.

Grelot, the artist, recounts again how a certain M. de Beaujeu, a knight of Malta, after 16 years of internment in the Seven Towers (the prison for persons of rank), broke out by night and took to the sea chased by dogs, was hit on the head by the oar of a passing *caïque* and nearly drowned but managed to flounder on board the vessel of M. d'Aplemont, the French ambassador who was just then sailing for home; how the gaoler having on this occasion duly reported the escape, the ship was stopped at the Dardanelles by the Sultan's orders and a demand made for the surrender of the prisoner and how M. d'Aplemont returned a spirited reply that the first man who came on board to fetch his guest would swing from the yardarm, and finally, with his guns trained on the forts, bluffed his way through, the crew—as it happened to be Christmas Day—singing a mass on deck as they sailed down the straits.

Hakluyt too has preserved the account of "the woorthy enterprise of John Foxe in delivering 266 Christians out of captivitie of the Turkes," that stirring feat of an English ship's gunner who rescued himself and his friends from a living death after fourteen years in the galleys, of which fragments have already been quoted.

But the best and fullest history of a Christian's experiences as a prisoner in Turkey is one which was written in 1599 by a young Bohemian noble and translated into English in the middle of the last century by his lineal descendant the Rev. A. H. Wratislaw, Headmaster of Bury St Edmunds Grammar School.

Baron Wencelaus Wratislaw (for such was the young man's name) was, to use his own words, "entrusted by my relatives to the care of Frederic Kregwitz, who was sent to Constantinople with rich presents, in the year 1591, by his Majesty the Roman Emperor Rudolph II, as Ambassador Extraordinary to the Turkish Emperor, Sultan Amurath III The object of my relatives was, that I should gain experience and see eastern countries."

After passing by Augsburg to buy jewellery as presents for the Turks, Herr von Kregwitz and his suite embarked in boats on the Danube, carrying their coaches with them, and rowed down to the frontier near Raab. Here they were met by a Turkish flotilla and towed on past Buda-Pesth (then a Turkish town) to Belgrade, whence they drove overland to Constantinople.

At Constantinople the embassy lived comfortably for some weeks, during which Baron Wratislaw made the most of his time by exploring the capital and getting into various scrapes. The Hungarian tribute, however, had just then fallen into arrear and Murad (to use the modern and more correct rendering of the Sultan's name) began to show himself very disagreeable.

The Grand Vizir was an ambitious old man named Sinan Pasha, who had started life as an Albanian swineherd, had been taken for an *ajami oghlan* and became a palace cook, from which post, having captured the Sultan's fancy, he had risen successively to be page, captain of janissaries, beylerbey, pasha and now ultimately Grand Vizir. It came presently to the ambassador's ears that Sinan, trading on the Sultan's cupidity, was working up for a war on Hungary and that secret preparations for a campaign were already in progress. Determined at all costs to give the Emperor warning, von Kregwitz at once began to employ secret agents to obtain information of the Turkish plans, and was so successful that after a time he actually had several of the vizirs and the *Sultan-valida* herself in his pay. The intelligence he thus obtained was kept in a secret place in the embassy vaults.

The Grand Vizir, growing suspicious, seized on the excuse of a fracas on the Hungarian frontier, in which some Turks had lost their lives, to intern the ambassador and his suite in their house, cutting them off from all communication with the outside world by placing a guard around and only allowing the inmates out to purchase food under a close escort. It happened just then that the embassy steward, one Ladislaw Mörthen by name, got into trouble with the ambassador, who locked him up in his own room as a punishment. Mörthen, indignant at this treatment, took the opportunity of the main door being opened to admit one of the janissaries, to break open his door and rush into the street shouting out that he was a convert to Islam. He was taken to Sinan, to whom he betrayed all that his master had been doing and told of the hidden papers.

The following day the Turks searched the embassy and found the incriminating documents. Von Kregwitz was taken away and apparently never heard of again. The fate of the others forms our present story, which from this point onwards shall be told in Wratislaw's own words, his narrative, which is somewhat diffuse in parts, being condensed within the necessary limits.

'After about two hours we saw people running from

all quarters by thousands to our house, placing themselves in rows, and creeping on the roofs, and at last
so many collected that we could not see to the end of them.
Not knowing what this indicated and what kind of spectacle was about to be exhibited, we imagined at first that
some part of our house was on fire; till, after a short time,
we saw the guard which was usually employed at executions making straight for our hotel. Behind this guard
rode the sub-pasha, the judges, the head-executioners,
heralds, and under-executioners, bearing fetters in their
hands. The eyes of all the people were then directed
upon us. When they arrived at the house, the sub-pasha
and the other Turks dismounted: the janissaries opened
our house with a noise and shout and led and dragged
all of us, wherever they could seize us, down the galleries and out of the house. They then opened the door,
and counted us out, one after the other, for they had a list
of us all. Then an executioner took each by his iron
ring, the sub-pasha mounted his horse, the guards began
to close round us, and make a way through the people.
As I could not stand upon my feet, they brought me a
Turk, whom they call a hamola, or porter, who carries
all manner of things from the sea about the city for hire,
on whose pannier, which was stuffed with rushes, they
perched me like a landrail, and I sat upon it like a dog
on a bank. [Wratislaw was suffering from dysentery at
the time.]

They led us, for greater disgrace and ridicule, through
the most populous squares and streets, and it was very
hot weather, so that we could have died for excessive
thirst. Some pitied us, others gnashed their teeth at us,
and said the best place we could go to was the gallows.
When they had led us up and down the city to their

satisfaction, they conducted us straight to the sand-gate, where the fish-market is held. On both sides of us, in front and behind, walked a countless multitude of people, for never before had so many persons been seen led to execution at once. Looking round I saw John von Winorz, the priest, and asked him where we were. He answered that we were not far from the gallows, and, therefore, had better resign ourselves to the Will of God, and commit our souls to Him. Meanwhile, we kept advancing further, the janissaries making a road for us by the use of their sticks. When I saw the hooks on the gallows, and two executioners upon it holding the pullies, I immediately lost my self-command, swooned, and became entirely unconscious. Nor did we expect aught else than that they would hang us all up, since that was exactly the course of proceeding which they observed with others at their execution.

My comrades related to me afterwards (for, as aforesaid, I had lost the power of thought and recollection, as well as sensation) that, when they brought us under the gallows, two more executioners climbed up, and meanwhile a judge addressed us to the following effect, telling us that we saw a terrible death before our eyes, and, therefore, for the great compassion which he felt for us, promised, by the head of the Sultan, his lord, that our lives should be granted us if we would but turn Mahometans. But, by the grace of God, none of us did this, but we were all ready to lose our lives in preference; although, on the other hand, we were so overwhelmed by fear of death that none of us knew whether he was alive or dead.

After remaining still for about a quarter of an hour, the sub-pasha gave orders to conduct us to the sea, which was close at hand. The vulgar, therefore, as they had not hung us on the hooks, had no other expectation but that they would drown us in the sea. Every living soul, therefore, ran down to the sea, and took their seats in boats and barges, for greater convenience in looking on. When they had brought us to the shore, they thrust us almost head-over-heels into a boat, in which camels and mules, with all manner of mercantile burdens are ferried over from Europe to Asia, cursing at us, meanwhile, vehemently, and pushing us in such a manner that the poor wretches pulled each other down by their chains. Coming to myself again, I thanked my God that it had pleased Him to release me from that terrible death. Having thrust off from the shore, the chief judge and his attendants sailed with us in the boat, and we had no other idea but that they would drown us, or take us to that frightful black tower, on the Black Sea, for they turned with us in that direction. Then they stopped and asked us again whether we were willing to become Turks, saying that it was now our last hour, as they were about to drown us all by Synan Pasha's orders ; that we should, therefore, have compassion on our youth, and that they were willing to make imperial gentlemen-in-waiting, spahis, and janissaries of us, and give us fine clothes and horses. But we constantly prayed to God, and, committing ourselves to Him, persevered in saying that whatever pleased His gracious Goodness should be our fate, acknowledging that we had deserved all this misery by our sins. We had spectators round us in thousands, who wished to gaze upon our watery funerals, for the upper and under executioners were also with the judge in our boat.

As soon as they saw our steadfastness, and that not

one of us would become a Turk, they threatened us, and angrily impressed upon us that they would put us into such a prison that, when there, we should wish to be dead rather than alive. After bullying us till they were satisfied, they brought us round at last to the imperial arsenal, or magazine, where there are many hundreds of various boats, and where stores of galleys, and other military requisites are kept in vaults. Having brought us to this place, the judges presented letters or orders from Ferhat Pasha to the Quardian Pasha, instructing him how we were to be dealt with. After this the executioners took the chains and rings off our necks, and two or three of them ran up, and tripped up the feet of each, so that he fell on the ground. Here we poor wretches expected that they would beat us with a stick, but, thank God, that did not take place; but gipsy smiths came, and putting an iron ring round the feet of one who lay on the ground, passed a chain through it, clinched it on an anvil, and then fastened a second, whom he selected, by the foot to the same chain. Seeing that this was all they did, each of us had himself coupled to the companion whom he liked best. As soon as two were coupled together, they were obliged to go immediately into the common prison. Not knowing to whom else to have myself fettered, I looked at our chaplain, my countryman, and asked him to have me fettered to him.

In this prison there are three buildings. In the principal building there are captives of various nations, artizans who construct galleys, and divers other things; for instance, carpenters, joiners, smiths, ropemakers, sailclothmakers, locksmiths, and coopers, who are conducted every day into this or that workshop. These are the best off of all, for they have it in their power to filch things, sell them secretly, and buy something to eat : nay, when they work industriously, porridge is given them on Friday, (the Turkish Sunday), and, above all, they have hopes of release before the rest. Such prisoners as are priests, scribes, scholars, citizens, or gentlemen, are in the greatest misery, because they have not learnt any handicraft, and no value is set upon them.

The second prison is for common prisoners who know no handicraft. Of these there were then about 700 persons, of all the various nations that there are beneath the sky. These are taken in the beginning of spring, on board the galleys as rowers. When they return from the voyage they must hew stone and marble, construct earthworks, carry materials for building, and in a word, like day-labourers, if there is any contemptible work to be done anywhere, they must perform it. They receive from one year's end to another nothing more for food than two loaves of bread per diem, and water to drink. The Turks strike and beat them like cattle for the least misconduct. Nay, not even at night do they enjoy repose, but must go to work if anybody wants them.

The third building is a hospital, in which the sick prisoners lie, and where the old men who are past work through age loiter about. These, besides bread, receive soup and porridge. This building is called Paul's prison. As long as they are there they are made comfortable; when they get well, they must work to make up what has been neglected; if they die, they are given to the prisoners to be buried, or thrown into the sea.

There were then but few prisoners in the gaol, for they had gone as rowers on board the war-boats, but they were from time to time expected. They at length returned from rowing on board the vessels of war, and came into the gaol amongst us. Learning that we had a priest amongst us, they treated him very reverentially, and went all before the superintendent of the guard, and humbly besought him to allow them on certain days, which were hallowed among Christians, to perform Divine Service before daylight and before they went to their work. They offered to give him a present for this permission, which was, accordingly, granted them.

Many years ago there had been an altar in the common prison, consecrated by a regular bishop, and fenced round with rails; and the prisoners possessed, also, a silver cup and the other requisites for the celebration of holy mass. On every great and apostolical festival our chaplain, who was temporarily released from his chains, celebrated holy mass, while I, with the chain, acted as acolyte, sang the epistle, and gave the prisoners the crucifix to kiss. They contributed alms according to their poverty, so that we always had a kreutzer or so by us for food, and were easily able to support ourselves. After mass the Turkish gipsies fettered the chaplain to me again by the chain.

Once, on a festival after holy mass, a master-carpenter, a Christian prisoner, invited the chaplain and me to partake of a fine tabby tom-cat, which he had fed up for a long time and named Marko. It was a fine and well-fatted cat, and I saw, with my own eyes, when the carpenter cut his throat. As my partner, Mr Chaplain, would not go, and fettered together as we were I could not go without him, he sent us, as a present, a fore-shoulder of the cat, which I ate. It was nice meat, and I enjoyed it very much, for hunger is a capital cook, so that nothing makes one disgusted; and if I had only had plenty of such tom-cats, they would have done me no harm.

At this time news arrived that our friends had obtained a glorious victory over the Turks in Hungary, and cut to pieces many thousands of them. On hearing this we were again in great terror, for the Turks looked sour at us, gnashed their teeth, and threatened to have us hung on the hooks. Then came the imperial kihaja, had us all called out, and said that they would cut off our noses and ears, because our friends, brothers, and cousins had slain so many Mussulmans.

The pasha of the guard then came to our prison, bringing with him two barbers, or hair-cutters, had us all summoned out, and ordered us all to sit down on the ground. We all wept, and entertained no other idea but that it would be done as we had been told, and, therefore, no one was willing to be the first to sit down, until the scourge compelled us so to do. Anybody can imagine how we, at this time, felt about the region of the heart. We were all as pale as a sheet, and the barbers, stepping up and seeing us so frightened, laughed heartily, and all our stomachs began to ache. When we had seated ourselves on the ground, instead of cutting off our noses and ears, they shaved our heads and beards with a razor, for some of us had their hair and beard grown to a considerable length, and, after laughing at us to their heart's content, bade us go back to prison. When our terror passed away, and we looked at and saw each other all clipped round and beardless, like so many calves' heads, we could not help laughing, because we could scarcely recognise one another. Neither did we bear them any malice for the state of baldness to which they had reduced us, and they were satisfied with having frightened us abundantly about nothing. Afterwards more trustworthy Turks informed us that the grand vizier had really ordered our noses and ears to be cut off, and ourselves to be sent, thus shamefully handled, to Christendom; but the mufti, their chief bishop, on learning it, had opposed it, and would not allow that maltreatment to be inflicted upon us, as we had not waged war against them, but had only been attached to an embassy, and were in no wise in fault; at any rate, he said, it would have been a sin to maltreat us thus. The grand vizier, not being able to revenge himself upon us in any other way, had our heads and beards shaved with a razor, and the next day all of us chained to the oars amongst the other prisoners on board the galleys.

We were conducted on board the galley, or large war-boat, under the care of a vigilant guard, and Achmet, the reis, or captain, who commanded on board the vessel, a Christian born in Italy, but who had now become a Turk, immediately received us and ordered us all to be chained to oars. The vessel was tolerably large, and in it five prisoners sat on a bench, pulling together at a single oar. It is incredible how great the misery of rowing in the galleys is; no work in the world can be harder: for they chain each prisoner by one foot under his seat, leaving him so far free to move that he can get on the bench and pull the oar. When they are rowing, it is impossible, on account of the great heat, to pull otherwise than naked, without any upper clothing, and with nothing on the whole body but a pair of linen trousers. When such a boat sails through the Dardanelles, out of the narrow into the broard sea, iron bracelets, or rings, are immediately passed over the hands of each captive, that they may not be able to resist and defend themselves against the Turks. And thus fettered hand and foot the captive must row day and night, unless there is a gale, till the skin on the body is scorched like that of a singed hog, and cracks from the heat. The sweat flows into the eyes and steeps the whole body, whence arises excessive agony, especially to silken hands unaccustomed to work, on which blisters are formed from the oars and yet give way with the oar one must; for when the superintendent of the boat sees any one taking breath, and resting, he immediately beats him, naked as he is, either with the usual galley-slave scourge, or with a wet rope dipped in the sea, till he makes abundance of bloody weals over his whole body.

Frequently some jackanapes of a rascally Turkish boy amuses himself with beating the captives from bench to bench one after the other, and laughing at them. All this you must not only bear patiently from the snivelling rascal, and hold your tongue, but, if you can bring yourself to it, you must kiss his hand, or foot, and beg the dirty boy not to be angry with you.

For food nothing is given but two small cakes of biscuit, but when they sail to some island where Christians live, you can sometimes beg, or, if you have money, buy yourself a little wine, and sometimes a little porridge, or soup. So too, when we rested one, two, three, or more days by the shore, we knitted gloves and stockings of cotton, sold them, and sometimes bought ourselves additional food, which we cooked ourselves in the vessel. Each of us had two blue shirts and a reddish blouse—there were no other upper clothes, but we only dressed ourselves in them at night. Indeed, we had a most miserable, sorrowful life, and worse than death, in that vessel.

Sometimes a draught of wine, which grows on the island Alla Marmora, where they hew marble, and is very good, cheered and strengthened us amidst this torture. We likewise enjoyed the good Wallachian cheese.

Six of us who were in partnership, having sold the gloves and stockings which we had made, bought a tolerably large piece of this cheese mixed with hair, which certainly came to us very acceptably, and tasted to us then better than macaroons; for we made soup of it, crumbled our mouldy biscuit into it, and eat it with remarkable appetite, paying no attention to and feeling no disgust at the circumstance that there were hairs in it. Ah! how many times, and indeed times out of number, did I remember, how in Bohemia they made soup of fine and good cheese even for useless greedy dogs, crumble fine bread into it, and give it them to eat; whereas, I, poor wretch, must thankfully receive such miserable hairy cheese and mouldy biscuit, and suffer hunger! Often did I wish, that, in point of food, I might be a companion to those dogs!

Once too a Turk brought us a bag of boiled sheep's heads for sale and we bought the heads from him and thanked him besides.

When we had already been half-a-year at the galleys, the Turks became fearful lest some of us should escape, and conducted us all back again from the galleys to our first prison, where they left us about a week.

Intelligence was again brought that our men had gained a glorious victory over the Turks in Hungary, whence great sorrow and lamentation arose on all sides;

and the clerk of the prisoners, Alfonso di Strada, a Spaniard, who had gained his liberty by work and service, came to us early in the morning, and sorrowfully informed us that the Turks were violently enraged with us, and in short, were on the point of putting us in the Black Tower.

After dinner the pasha's kihaja ordered us to be all called out, and made known to us the will of his pasha, and also bade us take our things and follow him, saying that we were to sail to the Black Tower. As soon as we heard the Black Tower mentioned, and received the unhappy news that we were to be placed in so gloomy a prison, we all with one voice began to weep and lament, till our hearts were breaking. All the other prisoners pitied us too, and wept with us; moreover, we would rather have undergone death than go to so unendurable a prison. Having, therefore, tied up our things in wallets, and each taking his own property on his shoulders, we mournfully bade adieu to the prisoners, but were unable to speak for excessive weeping. All who were in the prison accompanied us with tears and lamentations to the gate. One prisoner gave us half a loaf of bread as a parting gift, another some sewing needles, another a piece of cotton, and each what he had. When we came to the gate, and thus sorrowfully weeping, thanked the Quardian Pasha of the place for having been kind to us, he too wept over us with compassion.

Thus we got into the boat, not with tears, but with great moaning. When we drew near the fortress where the Black Tower is, the Turks pointed it out to us, comforting us and bidding us have hope in God, saying that He was mighty and could release us from it, as

The Black Sea entering in to the Thracian Bosphorus

EASTERN ENTRANCE TO BOSPHORUS (the site of the "Black Tower")

From George Sandys' *Travels*, 1632

indeed half-a-year before the prisoners had got out of
it; but we could neither speak nor look for weeping
and anguish, and it is wonderful where so many tears
stow themselves away in the eyes.

As soon as we ran ashore under the fortress itself
a ladder was let down to us, up which, each carrying
his wallet on his shoulders, we walked into the fortress
after our reis, or captain. On approaching the great
iron gates, which were opened to us, we saw a square
with a gallery round it reaching to the tower itself,
which was entered by an iron door. The captain of
our boat handed to Mehemet, the aga, or governor, of
the Black Tower, a letter from the chief pasha, on
perusing which the aga said with a loud voice:—"What
am I to do with these poor prisoners? They have not
deserved so severe a prison. Is there no less severe
prison to be found for them? It is not just to punish
guiltless people thus." And looking at us, for we were
all weeping from the bottom of our hearts, and had
our eyes bloodshot from weeping, he said:—"Allah
Buickter, kurtulur Siue!" i.e. "Fear not, God is a
mighty liberator[1]." He then ordered that terrible door
to be opened, and bade us go into the tower.

The tower is very lofty, but not very wide, so that
two-and-twenty of us and the first four, that is, six-and-
twenty persons, could scarcely lie down alongside of
each other; and, indeed, could not help touching each
other. Inside the tower is a thick oaken lattice, like a
cage in which lions are kept, so conveniently constructed that the guards can walk inside round the
lattice within which the prisoners sit, and see what they

[1] The *agha's* words were probably "*Allah buyuk dir qurtarir sizi,*"
i.e. "God is great. He will deliver you."

are doing. In the middle of this cage burns, day and night, a glass lamp, and round are stumps, or blocks, on which we supported our feet. We were, indeed, to have had our feet fastened in these blocks, but, as it pleased God to grant us to find favour in the eyes of the governor, he did not put us into the blocks, except when Turks whom he did not know were to come to the tower, when he sent guards in first with orders to put both our feet into the blocks and fasten us in. On the departure of the Turks he used to order us to be let out again.

This governor had been a Christian child, born in Croatia, and was then more than ninety years old; zealous in his religion, and compassionate towards us, but careful in his duties. He looked to the guards himself, came frequently into the tower, and had the fetters examined every day. Every week the guards examined all our clothes over the whole body, to see whether they could find a knife or file on any one, and, taking warning from the aga who had been hung, he did not allow his diligence to relax in the least.

When the third day came, and neither bread nor other food was given us, we sent for our aga, and asked what they wanted to do with us. And it being already the third day since we had had anything in our throats, if they wanted to kill us with hunger, we bade them throw us into the sea and drown us, that we might, at any rate, be quit of our misery. When we wept before him, he had such compassion on us that tears fell from his eyes, and he said to us :—" As God lives, and his great prophet Mahomet, I do not wish you so grievous and gloomy a prison ; and I cannot wonder sufficiently why they imprison you, and give no orders what is to

be done with you further. I do not think that they are
going to kill you with hunger, for surely they would
not have put you among the other prisoners; but you
would have been put into a vault, where they kill the
other Turks with hunger. Therefore, I will go immediately to Constantinople, and ascertain, and inform
you directly, what is to happen with you further." All
of us then kissed his hand, his clothes, and 'his feet,
recommended ourselves to his care with tears, and
waited in great terror for his arrival.

Returning before evening from Constantinople, he
comforted us by telling us that they were not going to
kill us, and declared that he had obtained orders to the
effect that three aspers, or kreutzers, a-day should be
given to us to live upon by the pasha, adding also as
follows:—"Since ye still have to wait long for the
payment, for the wages of court officials and soldiers
are paid quarterly, and your pensions will be paid then,
I must, therefore, provide you with means of support
in the interval." And these he provided as follows.
Knowing we could not wait for the money, like a good
man, he made himself our surety to the bakers in the
town by the Black Tower, arranging that they should
give each of us two loaves of bread daily, and he would
pay them the money every quarter. He also kept his
promise, for at the conclusion of the quarter he paid
the bakers, and kept for himself the third kreutzer per
diem for his trouble, though certainly he said that they
refused to give us more than two aspers, a sum which
we were obliged to receive thankfully. And since the
salt sea-water could not be drunk, they brought good
water from a spring on a hill some hours from the town,
and gave us two pitchers of it daily, so that, hot as it

was in our prison, we could scarcely quench our thirst, and often quarrelled together for the water, when one drank more of it than another. Therefore, that there might be equality amongst us, we took up the stocking trade, and made partnerships of five or six persons in each—one spinning the cotton, another winding it together, a third knitting, and so forth. When we had earned some money by selling what we had knit (for sometimes they sent us for it meal, oil, bread, vinegar, and even some aspers), we all clubbed together and bought as many mugs as there were persons, and also a large wooden tub, in which we set our mugs, and when the water was brought we filled them one after the other, till we had all had our turn ; but when there was any water remaining in the tub each took it for a day in turn, and kept it for himself in a large pitcher.

We bought ourselves, moreover, a large pot, and plastered it with clay, which our guards brought us, and made a kind of oven of it. We also bought coals and a bag with the proceeds of our knitting, and being already in partnership by fives and sixes, and having saved several pitchers of water, each had to boil and act in turn as cook for a week ; that is to say, taking a small loaf and two or three pieces of bread he crumbled them into the water, got up the fire, boiled the porridge, and gave it to his fellow-craftsmen to eat. The porridge was extremely nice, especially when at times we procured some olive oil, made it rich for ourselves, and licked our fingers afterwards.

When we had got used to the frightful darkness, and had formed this arrangement together, we obtained some Latin and German books, that is to say, the Bible, poems, and legends ; and whenever our guards

were changed we concluded that it was day, and all
sang a morning hymn, and read a legend, praying to
the Lord God for our release, and for the victory of
the Christians over the Turks; after which each turned
to his work and worked all day. In the evening, when
they had examined our fetters, we again sang an
evening hymn, and, after performing our devotions,
concluded that it was night, and betook ourselves to
repose, or read a brief hour by the light of the lamp.
It was, indeed a great comfort that we obtained those
books, and read to each other. The Turks certainly
laughed at our singing and praying, but they offered
us no hindrance therein, and when the time of their
own devotions came they observed it also.

When we had been more than four quarters of a
year in this Black Tower, with only one shirt and one
rug a-piece, the violent frosts and cold wet west-winds
tormented us in winter, just as much as the great heat
had done in summer, and therefore our aga made us
each a coat of cloth, in which we clad ourselves and
kept out the cold.

Being all emaciated with hunger, our guards begged
for us, from the fishermen, a large fish, just like a
round table, and with a long tail, which the Turks call
a *kedy baluk*, or cat-fish. This fish is not eaten, but
its fat, for it is very fat, is melted down. Our guards
begged this fish, which had been caught in the sea, from
the fishermen, and when they gave it us we received it
with great gratitude, and asked them to cut it in pieces
for us. When they had done as we wished, we were off
with several pieces immediately to the pot, boiled some,
baked the rest, and breakfasted off it with remarkably
good appetites, though afterwards we paid for it bitterly.

For we ate this fish's fat, and drank water after it, till our stomachs and bellies swelled, so that for many weeks we did not rise from our places. We informed our aga that we were seriously ill and that death awaited us. He came amongst us and, seeing our condition, vehemently reproached the Turks and threatened to punish them for poisoning us; he also strictly forbad anything to be given us without his knowledge. They, nevertheless, gave us snails and tortoises, which we boiled and ate with a good appetite. Neither did they do us any harm, for we had fortified our stomachs with hunger, and digested everything well, with the exception of that nasty cat-fish.'

At this stage of Wratislaw's imprisonment important outside events took place which reacted strongly on his fortunes, but which for our present purpose may be very briefly summarised as follows. In the first place the Turks won a notable success by capturing the town of Raab (half-way between Buda-Pesth and Vienna) from the Emperor. Almost immediately afterwards the Sultan died and was succeeded by Mohammed III. Sinan Pasha having won great kudos by the victory at Raab retained the Grand Vizirate under the new Sultan, and at once began preparations for another campaign, which was to prove disastrous to Turkey owing to the revolt of the subject principalities of Moldavia and Wallachia (the modern Rumania) and Transylvania. In his absence a certain Ibrahim acted as his *Kaimmakam*, or deputy, at Constantinople.

After this necessary parenthesis, the story shall be resumed as Wratislaw himself tells it.

CHAPTER XVI

A PRISONER IN THE GALLEYS AND
THE BLACK TOWER.

(2)

'On one occasion Ibrahim invited the Sultan to his gardens, on learning which our aga came to us, shouting: "Good news, Christians! good news! The most mighty Sultan makes an excursion tomorrow to Ibrahim's gardens. Therefore when a cannon is fired on the tower, shout with all the voice you have, and wish the Emperor prosperity and victory over his enemies."

In the morning the Sultan issued magnificently from his palace and sailed along the shore past the tower where we were in a boat gilded all over, as our guards told us. When he passed the tower the Turks fired heavy artillery. As soon as they ceased firing, we all called out and shouted with a loud voice, wishing him prosperity, our guards also assisting us in so doing. The Emperor heard the noise, but could not understand anything. When the Emperor sailed gently on, and the shouting increased more and more the farther he went, he asked what the noise was, and whence it came. Then the Lord God raised up a friend for us, Bostangi Pasha, the grand superintendent of the gardens, who stood behind the Emperor, and commanded the guard in the stern of the boat, and he said to the Emperor: "This voice, most gracious Emperor, is that of poor prisoners, who have now been long in yon tower, and

see not the light of the sun ; they are calling and beg-
ging for mercy." The Emperor stopped, and asked
what manner of prisoners they were. Information was
given him that they were the servants of the ambassador
of the Viennese king, who had been sent to his father,
Sultan Amurath, with the annual gift and handsome
presents, and that their lord had been a traitor, and
had written down all manner of intelligence for his king ;
also that Synan Pasha had commanded him to be put
to death in prison, and his suite to be placed in that
tower, and that, though guiltless, they had already been
three years imprisoned in irons.

Upon this the Emperor said : "Since they are guiltless prisoners, and have never drawn the sword against
us, it is not a proper thing to afflict them by imprisonment ; therefore, I command that they be released."
He then went on his way. Then the kind Turks and
guards who heard this ran tumbling over each other to
us, hoping to receive presents for telling us some very
good news. And when we promised them, they informed
us that their Emperor had given orders to set us at
liberty. Then, being filled with boundless joy, we distributed to them everything that we had, rugs, clothes,
and spirits, and kissed and embraced each other, not
imagining but that we should be set free in the morning.
But we were shamefully deceived. For there in heathen-
dom, just as with us Christians, when the Emperor
makes any promise to any one, if that person has not
a good friend at court, and if he makes no presents, his
just matter is often left in the lurch. Thus it happened
to us poor wretches. For having given away everything
that we possessed, we had afterwards to suffer hunger
and all manner of want ; and whereas we might have

lain on the rugs, we were obliged to be satisfied with
the bare ground.

News now arrived that Synan Pasha had returned
to Constantinople and having appeased the Emperor
for the losses of his army was received into high favour.
After this our allowance of two aspers each was not
paid for a whole quarter, and our aga went to court and
mentioned us to the vizier, who answered angrily that
he would have us flayed alive, and our skins made into
drums. This was told us sorrowfully by the aga, who
bade us entreat God that the vizier's anger might be
appeased.

Presently our men and the Transylvanians took
some fortresses from the Turks and slew a good many.
Whereupon the Turks immediately prepared for war
and Synan was proclaimed commander-in-chief. Since
he had been so unfortunate in the previous year he
used every exertion to prevail upon the Sultan to march
into Hungary in person, and when through his and the
soldiers' urgency the Emperor was inclined to go, he
had all manner of military engines prepared, everything
requisite for an imperial campaign got ready and the
soldiers mustered. But through his great exertions a
dysentery suddenly attacked him and he died.

At that time very cold and disagreeable north winds
began to blow and many of us fell very sick, so that
we longed to die being utterly enfeebled by hunger and
tortured by the intolerable darkness, for we had no hope
of getting out of the tower unless peace were made
between our Emperor and the Sultan.

While we were thus mournfully lamenting and singing sad songs, and had lost all hope of quitting the
tower till death, in comes our aga amongst us, with a

cheerful countenance, bidding us give him a reward, because he was about to tell us good news. Waking up, as it were from sleep, we all crowded round him, like chickens round a hen, beseeching him to tell us the good news, kissing his feet, hands, and clothes. Not having the heart to refuse our request, he informed us that Ibrahim Pasha was chosen grand vizier, and gave us good hope of our release. On hearing this, without having had any expectation of it, we raised our hands and thanked God heartily, and asked the aga to advise us what we should do, for we scarce knew what to do for joy. For in truth, if a man has not experienced misery, want, hunger, cold, heat, and grievous imprisonment, he cannot possibly believe one who has been in such a condition. He advised us to send a petition to the pasha, and wish him prosperity in his new office, long life, and victory over his enemies, promising to deliver the petition to the pasha and to intercede for us. In return for this we kissed his hands and feet for joy, and promised to give him much more; and having given the writing to a Turkish priest to copy out, we sent it to the aga to look over, committing ourselves to the Lord God and to him. He got into his caique, or six-oared boat, and going to Constantinople, first wished Ibrahim joy of his new office, and then delivered the writing from us.

The pasha received our letter and said: "Dear aga, thou perceivest and knowest how great a burden is placed upon me, so that I have more cares than hairs in my beard. Therefore, it is impossible to attend to them before I set more important matters in order. Remind me in about two or three weeks' time, and conduct them to the divan (the national council) and

I will use every means that they may be freed from this imprisonment." When the aga made this known to us we were filled with great joy, and waited anxiously for the time to come.

When the longed-for time came, the aga gave orders for us all to be let out of the tower, and the fetters to be taken off one foot. These we tied to our girdles, that we might carry them the more easily. On coming into the open air we were refreshed, as if born anew; yet we could not look at the sun, but, on coming suddenly out of such great darkness into the light, tears streamed from our eyes, till they became accustomed to it again. Meanwhile the aga ordered the caique to be prepared for us to sail to Constantinople; and on looking over us, and seeing me, the youngest of all, with long hair and no beard, pale and emaciated, he said that I should stay there below with the guards and walk about, till he returned with my comrades, otherwise, on account of my youth, I might easily be seized by some pasha and forced to turn Mahometan.

Wishing with my whole heart to make the excursions and see Constantinople, I kissed the aga's hand, and besought him, for God's sake, to take me also with him. He said to me: "If thou wilt have it so, thou shalt come with us; but I do not promise thee that thou wilt return." Thus we got into the boat and sailed to Constantinople, landed from the boat, and went into the city, where a great concourse of the Turkish mob surrounded us, asking who and whence we were? But our aga answered them himself, and forbad us to say a word. Having very long hair flowing over my shoulders, and being beardless, I was the most tormented; for one pulled me by the hair, another stared in my face, a third talked to me, and asked me who I was; but the aga seeing this, and fearing for me, did not venture to take me into the divan: but going to the church of St Sophia, left me there with two Turks, under a projection of the roof, where some lime was lying, and ordered me to sit down on the ground, that the Turks going that way might not see me.

When my companions entered the divan, all the pashas present arose, went to the Sultan, and made intercession that we might be released from prison, saying that peace would be made between the Emperors so much the sooner. But orders were given to our aga to place us again in the tower, and bring me also, if I were still alive, to the divan in a fortnight. The prisoners, my comrades, thanked the pashas, and returned towards the Black Tower, past the church of St Sophia, where I sat in the lime-vault. I crawled out of the lime-vault and joined them with my two guards, and we went to the tower, and anxiously waited for the last day of the fortnight.

After a fortnight we all sailed again to Constantinople with one fetter. On going into the divan we were informed, through an interpreter, that the mighty Sultan, out of his natural goodness, released us all from so grievous an imprisonment, and counselled us to show gratitude in return, and never to wage war against him; otherwise, if any of us were seized and captured in war, he would be immediately impaled. Likewise, when we returned to our own country, he bade us, with the aid of our friends, bring it to pass that our king should seek peace from the mighty Sultan, and that the prisoners on both sides should be released. Upon this they inscribed us by name in the record books, and all of us, falling at the feet of the pashas, wished to kiss them, which, however, they did not permit, and, thanking them for their great kindness, promised that none of us (knowing their great power and might) would serve in war to the day of our death; but that, as soon as we arrived in Christendom, we would in every wise counsel our Emperor and our friends to humble themselves to the Sultan, and seek peace from him, and that we knew that negotiations for peace would be begun as soon as we informed them of such enormous preparations.

There were also there present the ambassadors of the King of France and the Queen of England, who were to follow the Turkish army to the city of Erlau, and to whom several camels and horses had been assigned, and also a chiaous appointed, with twenty janissaries, to protect them and prevent the Turkish multitude from injuring them in aught. These ambassadors befriended us, and entreated that we might be freed from prison immediately, and sent to Christendom by sea, by way of Venice. That request being made, the ambassadors and we were commanded to leave the council, and, after a short time, the pashas summoned the English ambassador, and bade him, whenever he should follow the Sultan, to take us under his protection, and provide for us, as far as Greek Belgrade. They then assigned us thirty-five camels and four carriages, to put our baggage on, and also ride on ourselves; and also promised to give us five tents and six janissaries for our safety, and meanwhile commanded us to depart to the tower, take our necessaries (*i.e.* our rags), and wait upon the English ambassador.

Some days later we were released by the gipsy smiths from our irons and fetters, and could not sleep all night long for joy, but tied our rags together, distributed something to the poor prisoners who remained there after us, and bade adieu to them ; for the poor fellows wept bitterly, knowing that they were to remain still longer in that miserable prison, and must almost despair of their freedom.

These miserable prisoners begged us, if we reached Christendom, to entreat our Emperor on their behalf, that they might be freed from that cruel tower by the exchange of other Turks for them. This we promised to do.

Next day we bade adieu to them with great weeping, and quitted, on the festival of St Peter and St Paul, that most gloomy Black Tower, in which we had been shut up two years and five weeks without intermission, and going to the aga, thanked him and the rest of the guards for the kindness and favour that they had shown us, and promised (and also afterwards fulfilled our promise) to send them handsome knives, and the aga a striking-clock. The aga then had us conducted to the English ambassador at Galata, who received us in a friendly manner, and ordered a bath to be prepared for us, that we might be cleansed from the filthy condition in which we were. After the bath we visited the Catholic churches, of which there are seven in Galata, and gave thanks to the Lord God for our deliverance, from so exceeding cruel an imprisonment, fervently beseeching Him to be our Guide and Gracious Protector to our own dear country.

About that time Sultan Mehemet marched with great pomp from Constantinople, with all his court and his principal warriors, and having had tents pitched before the city, rested there several days according to custom, waiting for more soldiers. For several pashas from Egypt, Palestine, Cairo, and other lands beyond sea, were still marching up with their armies, and they were waiting for them.

When the Sultan had marched with the main army, the beglerbeg of the land of Greece pitched his tent with the rest of the army, about 80,000 strong, in the same place where the Emperor had previously been, and rested there two days. The English ambassador stayed with us, two days at Galata, and on the third day we marched in good order with these 80,000, always pitching our tents where the Emperor had rested for the night. When we arrived at Greek Belgrade, the whole army was concentrated together.

The Emperor would not lodge in the castle, but lay in the open country; and some thousand Tatars also joined him, who day and night were burning the villages of Christians living under the protection of the Turks, and driving herds of cattle, and droves of unbroken mares into the camp. These Tatars obtained such an abundance of cattle that they sold two Hungarian oxen for a dollar, more or less, and cows for twenty or thirty aspers the pair. We, too, bought a calf from under a cow for eight aspers, and eat meat to our heart's content.

Meanwhile the English ambassador made application to Ibrahim Pasha to send us to Buda and set us at liberty, because he wished to write to our Emperor about making peace. He also procured us access to him and the aga in command of the janissaries, and when we were admitted into his presence in his tent, we kissed his feet, and besought him to set us free before the mighty Sultan marched to Erlau, because eventually, our Emperor, owing to us, would send off commissioners to humble themselves to the Sultan in his stead, and sue for peace. He replied that we should be set free but that we were to remember the kindnesses shown us, noise their great forces abroad everywhere, and induce the Christians to make peace before they arrived at Erlau. And if our Emperor wished to send any of us to the Turkish emperor to negotiate such a peace, we were not to fear aught, but boldly and willingly to make ourselves useful in the matter, he swearing by the beard of the Sultan, his lord, that no harm should happen to us, but that we should be presented with distinguished gifts, handsome clothes and horses, and dismissed in safety to our own country.

When we had promised all this and much more, a letter credential and emancipatory was given us, and also one to the pasha at Buda (five of our party having been in a tower there ever since the death of my lord the resident), to the effect that he was to release them from prison, and entrust us to boatmen, to go to a fortress of our own up the Danube. In return for this kindness we all fell at his feet and thanked him. It was our great good fortune, that we received the letter to the pasha at Buda, and the letter credential that day, for, had it not happened so, we should certainly have all been cut in pieces, as will soon be related.

When we arrived at Zolnak we heard news that our people had taken the fortress of Hatwan from the Turks, and that the Walloons had behaved like dogs, not like Christians, to the Turks torturing them and killing their wives and children so that it was grievous to hear the lamentations of the Turks, who affirmed that it was the Germans who had exercised such cruelty. In this ill-

humour they cut their lately-captured prisoners in pieces
and wished to sabre even the Christian ambassadors,
and more especially us prisoners, and would have carried
this into execution had it not been, firstly, for the Divine
protection, and secondly, for Ibrahim Pasha and the
aga in command of the janissaries, who immediately
surrounded the whole place where the Christian ambassadors were living with us with a strong guard of
janissaries, and allowed no one to have access to us.
Orders were then given to us not to show ourselves to
any one, but to remain in our tent, and not to quit it
under pain of death.

As the Turks remained three days at Zolnak for
sorrow and never moved, our ambassador kept constantly applying to the pasha, through his chiaous, that,
according to his promise, fifty hussars, or Turkish archers,
should be assigned us, to escort us as far as Buda. But
the pasha was vehemently enraged, and threatened to
have us all put to the sword, asking whether it was in
return for this that he was to set us at liberty, because
our fathers, uncles, and brothers, had behaved so dis-
honourably to their dear friends the Turks at Hatwan?
Therefore, he bade him leave him quiet in the matter,
and not press him, if he did not wish to meet with something worse himself.

When the English ambassador sorrowfully made
known this sad intelligence to us, and said that we were
in danger of our lives, we were greatly terrified and
cast down. He also counselled us to pray fervently to
the Lord God, that, since it had pleased him to free us
from so grievous a prison, it might please Him to be
our God still further, and grant us a happy return to
our own dear country. And as he understood, that, as

soon as the camp moved, we might have some difficulty, and might even perhaps be put to the sword, he cared for us faithfully, hired four peasant carts to go to Buda, gave us 100 ducats for the journey, assigned us his own interpreter, and a janissary to guard us, and counselled us in God's name, as soon as the Emperor marched towards Erlau, to turn by another way towards Buda, since we already had our credentials and the letter to the Pasha of Buda.

As we were obliged to travel that night by a most dangerous road, where day and night the Turks and Tatars and our hussars were skirmishing—and, in fact, they brought into the camp daily captured heyduks of ours, and wounded hussars, and also multitudes of Christians' heads—we were constrained to swear to the janissary that, if Christians came upon us, no harm should happen to him, and he, on his part, promised in return that, if Turks came upon us, we should travel on in safety, since we had the Turkish emperor's passport; but he acknowledged that he could not make any promise for the Tatars if we fell into their hands, but said that he should be cut in pieces with us himself, for the Tatars did not even spare a Turk, but when they fall upon them by tens or twenties, and are more than a match for them, they sabre them, and plunder them of everything, without paying the least regard to any orders. For this reason we took a guide with us, and, after bidding adieu to the ambassador of the English queen, and thanking him for his great kindness, as soon as the Sultan moved from Zolnak towards Erlau we turned, with great terror, towards Buda, in the name of God.

As we went on our way we kept continually looking

back, with a timid and terrified heart, to see whether
they were pursuing us, and were in constant expectation
of being cut to pieces, since we were obliged to travel
through the most dangerous localities, where Turks,
Tatars, and Christians were skirmishing, it being impossible, as our guide informed us, to go by any other road.
Nevertheless it pleased a merciful God so to order it
that during the whole day, from morning dawn to
evening twilight, we never met a single human being;
only on arriving, when it was almost twilight, at a large
Hungarian village, we saw about a hundred Tatars
moving about the vineyards. Filled with terror, we
hastened to the village, which was entirely surrounded
by a moat, and besought the inhabitants to protect us
against the Tatars and admit us into the village, which
they did. The poor peasants threw a little bridge over
the moat, bade us sorrowfully welcome, and informed
us what excessive ill-treatment they were compelled
to endure from the Tatars, about 500 of whom were
encamped in the village. They, therefore, counselled
us to go without delay to the vicarage, and conceal ourselves somewhere, that the Tatars might not see us.
We listened to their advice, went to the vicar, and
begged him to open the church to us. He kindly gave
us cheese and slices of bread, and admitted us into the
church, where, with a contrite heart, we besought God
for mercy and protection against the Tatars. Not
knowing what plan to adopt, we also hoped in the
janissary, and trusted that our Turkish passport would
be available for us. But the janissary was as much
afraid of the Tatars as ourselves, and consequently
turned quite pale, and forbad us to speak to him in
Turkish.

Meanwhile the Tatars lighted large fires in the village, roasted oxen and sheep whole, cut off the cooked flesh, and ate like dogs. When we quitted the church, and began to feed our horses, the Tatars got intelligence of us, and immediately crowded to us, to the number of about 200, and, surrounding us, asked us who and what we were. We and the janissary made them a low Turkish obeisance, answered that we were going to Buda by order of the Sultan, and exhibited the Sultan's letters. But they replied, contemptuously, that it would be an improper thing to let us go, and sent for their captain, and the good God knows what they intended to do with us. Perceiving that it would not go well with us, and that we should either be made prisoners, or put to the sword by them, we prayed very penitently in heart, and besought God that it might please Him to be our protector, which, in fact, came to pass at sunset.

Wonder of wonders, and mighty power of God! Although the whole of that day had been very bright, the sun shining beautifully throughout, and not the least vapour or cloud had been visible, it nevertheless pleased a most merciful God, who never forsaketh them that trust in Him, to raise an exceedingly violent wind, and after it a tempest, so that it did not rain but pour, and a water-spout must have burst. The whole village and the trenches were filled with water, and the Tatars returned to their horses, the tempest having extinguished all their fires. During this violent tempest we harnessed our horses to the carriages, by the advice of the poor peasants, and quitted the village, taking with us a peasant to guide us by a route different from that which we had intended to pursue, as there were Tatars encamped in all the surrounding villages. This violent rain lasted without intermission till midnight, and during it we nevertheless travelled onwards, though we were obliged to pull the horses and carriages out of quagmires and help them forwards. We also travelled through a great number of burnt and forsaken villages, and heard the crying, weeping, and wailing of the poor people, and the lowing of the captured cattle. However, we made our way gradually onwards, for God strengthened our horses and ourselves, and arrived, about three hours before daybreak, at a heath, where we gave our horses hay and rested ourselves. But as soon as the horses had eaten a little we commenced our journey.

When day had fully dawned we heard loud salvos of artillery from Buda, which, at so great a distance, was surprising to us. It again occurred that no one met us on our journey till it was just noon, when we saw a large number of cavalry riding towards us on the plain. When they approached us we found that it was an exceedingly fine body of about 10,000 cavalry, with which the Pasha of Bosnia was on his way to reinforce the Sultan at Erlau. They all had long lances and various-coloured pennons upon them. As soon as they espied us about a hundred of them darted forwards, and rode at full gallop towards us with their lances in the rest.

As soon as our janissary knew that they were Turks, he dismounted, saluted them, and informed them who we were and whither he was conducting us. Our interpreter also rode with him to the pasha, showed him our letters, and informed him that the Sultan was already moving towards Erlau with his whole army.

He then returned to us again. When the pasha's army had passed us, we made for Pesth, and arrived at the city about an hour before sunset.

In the morning when the pasha of Pesth returned the Sultan's letter was delivered to him by us, in which orders were given him to escort us to the nearest Christian fortress, and set at liberty our five comrades, who had been in prison at Buda ever since the death of our ambassador. The pasha read the letter through, and not only immediately set our comrades at liberty, but also gave us plenty to eat and drink, and ordered boatmen to take us up stream to the fortress of Towaschow.

The next day, early in the morning, we sent the peasants, with the carriages and some of our things, forwards to Towaschow, requesting them to inform the Christian soldiers there of our liberation and arrival, and intending to recompense them there for the use of the carriages. But the poor fellows fell in with some Tatars and were put to the sword by them. We then got into a boat, and were pulled up stream, while our janissary and dragoman, or interpreter, rode on horseback along the bank. When we got close to Towaschow, we saw the bastions full of German soldiers, and imagined that our peasants had already made known our approach in the fortress. Such, however, was not the case. For a few days before some Turks, disguised in women's clothes, had sailed in a boat to the very skirts of the fortress, had seized and bound two fishermen and a woman, and had carried them off to Buda. Thus the people at Towaschow imagined that some more Turks were coming on a plundering expedition, and had disguised themselves like captives, in order the more easily to delude the Christians. Moreover, seeing the janissary and dragoman on the other bank of the Danube, they determined to allow us to approach the fortress within point-blank range of their cannon. Being then so close to the fortress, and not knowing what to do for joy, we began to embrace and kiss each other. At this moment our friends fired two pieces, one at the janissary, and the other at our boat, so that the water splashed over us, the artilleryman having fired a little too low. The boatmen, therefore, saw their danger, and wanted to let us fall again down stream. We prevented them from doing this, took the oars out of their hands, and raising a hat on the point of a spear, called out with a loud voice that we were Christians. The commander, Rosenhahn, a German by birth, saw this, and stepping up to the artilleryman, forbad him to fire any more, otherwise he would have shot our boat through with a second discharge, and we must have been drowned. In fact, I afterwards ascertained myself that he had taken better aim than the first time, and would certainly not have missed us.

Terrified as we were, we, nevertheless, approached the fortress, and calling out in German and Hungarian, made known who we were. Then there came to meet us a couple of boats, with two guns each, which first made a circuit round us, that we might not escape, and occupied the Danube behind us. They then rowed straight up to us, with their firearms cocked, and asked who we were. Upon our briefly informing them, they immediately lashed our boat to theirs, and pulled to the front of the fortress, where we got out, and all kneeling down, thanked God with heartfelt tears for our deliverance from so grievous an imprisonment.

In the morning we went in a boat to Gran where we begged to be conveyed to Vienna.

We arrived at Vienna, which was then under his grace the Archduke Maximilian, and were permitted to have an audience. We kissed his hand, and after giving him certain information about the Sultan's march, and the strength of his army, petitioned for pecuniary assistance to enable us to travel to Prague. We obtained our request, and he not only gave us money for the journey, but also ordered us to be conveyed to Prague to his brother, his Imperial Majesty Rudolph the Second.

When we arrived at Prague, and met our friends, O! it is impossible to describe the joy! His Majesty the Emperor, hearing of us, was graciously pleased to summon us to his presence. We kissed his hand and related how much we had had to endure in his service for all Christendom, and humbly entreated him to be our gracious emperor, king, and lord, and to be pleased to grant us some acceptable recompence for it. His majesty looked kindly upon us all, and said, in German,—" Wir wollen thun!" "We will do so!" It was then his pleasure to leave us; and, although orders were certainly given by him that a considerable sum of money should be divided amongst us, yet God knows in whose hands it remained; for 100, and 150 dollars, more or less, were given to some of us, who were foreigners, to enable them to reach their homes; whereas, after much entreaty, and many applications, nothing was given to us Bohemians, but merely the offer made that, if we liked to take service in the Emperor's court, we should take precedence of others. But we committed all to God, and preferred to return without money to our parents, friends, and acquaintances, who received us, as everybody can judge, with exceeding joy of heart. Thus, every one of us may, and ought to rejoice at this, and thank God, the best of comforters and succourers in sorrow, with heart and lips, to the day of his death. For, when all hope failed, all succour came to nought, and it seemed impossible to all men, both Turks and Christians, that we should return to our own country out of a prison so grievous, and, in all human judgment, so beyond the possibility of liberation, He set us at liberty by His mighty hand, to Whom, One true and living God in Trinity, be ascribed, honour, glory, and praise for ever and ever !'

The deliverance of Wratislaw and his companions was ultimately brought about, as we have seen, by the intervention of the English and French envoys, and their actual escape from Turkey was entirely due to the efforts of our own ambassador. However natural it may seem at the present day for a foreign ambassador to do all in his power for subjects of another Christian Power reduced to such a plight, one has only to remember how different the conditions were in the last decade of the sixteenth century to experience a real feeling of pride in our fellow-countryman's behaviour. The prisoners had failed in their appeal to their compatriots in Pera, whose refusal to advance even the sum needed to redeem the poor wretches from their vile durance in the Black Tower is an eloquent commentary on the existing standards of humanity. The English ambassador, meanwhile, was not only alien to the prisoners by birth and language, but—a greater bar still in those days of religious intolerance—he professed a different faith. In spite of this, and careless of the personal risk in befriending the subjects of a nation at war with Turkey, he first of all cajoled the Grand Vizir into letting the prisoners separate from the army and, when they started on their solitary journey, provided them with every material assistance in his power. If only on account of his great-hearted action on this occasion, he deserves a special mention in these pages.

Sir Edward Barton was, technically at least, the first ambassador from England to the Porte. William Harebone—whose voyage to Turkey in " The Great Susan " in 1582 is recounted in Hakluyt—had, indeed, preceded him as Queen Elizabeth's Agent at the Sultan's court, but it was Barton who first received the ambassadorial title after having already spent some half-a-dozen years at Constantinople. During those years, Murad IV had died, and had been succeeded, as already related, by Sultan Mohammed, who inaugurated his reign by killing off his nineteen brothers in one fell swoop, a " record " even in the bloody annals of the royal house. He displayed a paradoxical leniency towards slaves and Christian prisoners, one of his first sovereign acts being to emancipate the whole crew of the galley which brought him to the capital. Towards Sir Edward Barton he showed a good deal of kindness. He required him, however, to go with him on his military campaigns, and in one of his letters to the Queen of England he mentions that her "well-beloved ambassador" having been bidden by himself to follow the imperial camp, there not being time enough to obtain sanction from his royal mistress, had rendered services in the campaign which caused him (the Sultan) the greatest satisfaction. The strain of the frequent marches under war conditions finally broke Barton's health and, on his return from the campaign ending in the famous battle of Cerestes, he expired at his post from sheer exhaustion. His memory is preserved by a brass tablet in the Embassy chapel in Pera.

Turning again to the stories which we have of life and captivity among the Turks, it is remarkable how strongly they bring to light the religious constancy of the authors. Protestants and Roman Catholics alike appear as finding their main hope and comfort in the firm belief that they are the individual objects of divine interposition. Each hairbreadth escape from death at the hands of fanatical Turks or of " raging Tartarians," by sudden decapitation or by the lingering torture of the *gauch*, is duly ascribed to the protection of the Almighty and is followed invariably by a pious tribute of thanksgiving. The steadfastness of Christian captives and the palpable faith of such men as those, who, in the appalling surroundings of the arsenal prison, would sacrifice their infinitesimal gains to provide themselves with an altar and the necessary accessories for the celebration of mass, must surely have turned many a strict Turk to secret admiration of the religion which he was bound outwardly to spurn.

A perpetual reminder of the days when the sufferings of prisoners in Turkey were constantly present in men's minds exists still in the special intercession in the Litany framed originally in their behalf—and during the recent war restored awhile to its old significance :—
That it may please thee to have mercy on all prisoners and captives ; we beseech thee to hear us, good Lord.

All our characters have now passed across the stage, from the Sultan to the galley-slave, and, on the exit of this last, the curtain falls. The scenes have, perhaps, somewhat lacked cohesion, and chronology has been sadly ignored, but I have done my best to compound a whole which will tempt the reader's imagination to reconstruct a picture of old Turkey. A picture it will be of motley colours and fantastic outlines, a blending of East and West meeting for once on the common borderline and giving birth to as strange an outcrop of civilization as has ever flourished in the world's history.

GLOSSARY

Turkish and other foreign words which occur in this book, excepting
those whose meaning is given in the text

Asper. An old Turkish coin.

Bailo. Bailiff or diplomatic agent (Italian).

Caïque. A light build of boat, peculiar to the Bosphorus.

Capitulations. The early treaties between Turkey and the European
Powers by which the latter claim extensive extra-territorial rights, in
particular that of exercising jurisdiction over their nationals through
the Consular Courts. The Capitulations were still in force when war
broke out in 1914.

Divan. The Turkish Council of Ministers; also a long, low settee running
round the sides of a room.

Fetva. Legal decision or verdict pronounced by the *Sheikh-ul-Islam* or
other qualified doctor of Mohammedan theology and law.

Gauch. An instrument of torture and death, consisting of a scaffolding
set at intervals with large meat-hooks on to which the victim was
thrown from above, and, being impaled, was left to die slowly.

Ghiaour. An infidel (i.e., non-Mussulman).

Hajji. Pilgrim, a title retained for life by one who has made the pilgrimage
to Mecca.

Hoji. Corruption of the foregoing, or of *Hoja* (Khwája) = " Dominie " (a
schoolmaster or teacher).

Imam. A minor religious functionary who leads the faithful in prayer and
may have charge of a small mosque.

Jehad. Religious war.

Khan. Chieftain; also an inn.

Maidan. A large open space.

Maüna. A sailing boat resembling a dhow (from the Italian).

Mufti. An interpreter of Koranic law, from whom a *fetva* (see above) is
sought.

Oghlan. Boy.

Pashalik. A large administrative area, governed by a *Pasha*.

Pillau or *Pillaf.* A dish of boiled rice, spiced and garnished with various
delicacies.

Proveditore. A Venetian colonial governor or commander-in-chief.

Rayah. Christian subject of the Turks.

Sakka. Water carrier.

Sanjak. A small administrative area; also the official governing the same
(lit.: a flag).

Sanziacke. Corruption of foregoing.

Selamlik. Friday service at one of the mosques at the capital, attended
by the Sultan in state.

Seraglio. Palace (Italianized form of Turkish word *serai*).

Sofraji. Butler.

Sultan-valida. The mother of the reigning Sultan.

Tekyé. Monastery.

Top. A cannon.

Tufang. A gun.

Ulema (plural of the Arabic word *alim*). The body of "doctors" or pro-
pounders of the religious law (lit.: men of knowledge).

Zaïm. The holder of a *ziamet* or fief.

For EU product safety concerns, contact us at Calle de José Abascal, 56–1°,
28003 Madrid, Spain or eugpsr@cambridge.org.

www.ingramcontent.com/pod-product-compliance
Ingram Content Group UK Ltd.
Pitfield, Milton Keynes, MK11 3LW, UK
UKHW010035140625
459647UK00012BA/1394